T0220413

Spring REST

Building Java Microservices and Cloud Applications

Second Edition

Balaji Varanasi
Maxim Bartkov

Apress®

Spring REST: Building Java Microservices and Cloud Applications

Balaji Varanasi
Salt Lake City, UT, USA

Maxim Bartkov
Kharkov, Ukraine

ISBN-13 (pbk): 978-1-4842-7476-7
https://doi.org/10.1007/978-1-4842-7477-4

ISBN-13 (electronic): 978-1-4842-7477-4

Managing Director, Apress Media LLC: Welmoed Spahr
Acquisitions Editor: Steve Anglin
Development Editor: James Markham
Coordinating Editor: Mark Powers

Cover designed by eStudioCalamar

Cover image by Joel Holland on Unsplash (www.unsplash.com)

Distributed to the book trade worldwide by Apress Media, LLC, 1 New York Plaza, New York, NY 10004, U.S.A. Phone 1-800-SPRINGER, fax (201) 348-4505, e-mail orders-ny@springer-sbm.com, or visit www.springeronline.com. Apress Media, LLC is a California LLC and the sole member (owner) is Springer Science + Business Media Finance Inc (SSBM Finance Inc). SSBM Finance Inc is a **Delaware** corporation.

For information on translations, please e-mail booktranslations@springernature.com; for reprint, paperback, or audio rights, please e-mail bookpermissions@springernature.com.

Apress titles may be purchased in bulk for academic, corporate, or promotional use. eBook versions and licenses are also available for most titles. For more information, reference our Print and eBook Bulk Sales web page at http://www.apress.com/bulk-sales.

Any source code or other supplementary material referenced by the author in this book is available to readers on GitHub via the book's product page, located at www.apress.com/9781484274767. For more detailed information, please visit http://www.apress.com/source-code.

Printed on acid-free paper

Table of Contents

About the Authors..ix

About the Technical Reviewer xi

Acknowledgments xiii

Introduction xv

Chapter 1: Introduction to REST 1

What Is REST?...1

Understanding Resources..3

 Identifying Resources..3

 URI Templates..4

Representation...5

HTTP Methods...6

 Safety 6

 Idempotency..7

 GET 7

 HEAD..9

 DELETE...9

 PUT 10

 POST 12

 PATCH 13

HTTP Status Codes..14

Richardson's Maturity Model 16

 Level Zero...17

 Level One..17

 Level Two..18

 Level Three...18

Building a RESTful API...18

Summary...19

Chapter 2: Spring Web MVC Primer 21

Spring Overview...21

    Dependency Injection 23

    Aspect-Oriented Programming..23

Spring Web MVC Overview...24

    Model View Controller Pattern 24

    Spring Web MVC Architecture..25

    Spring Web MVC Components 27

Summary...44

Chapter 3: RESTful Spring 45

Generating a Spring Boot Project..46

    Installing a Build Tool..46

    Generating a Project Using start.spring.io..48

    Generating a Project Using STS..56

    Generating a Project Using the CLI...62

Accessing REST Applications...63

    Postman 64

    RESTClient...65

Summary...66

Chapter 4: Beginning QuickPoll Application 67

Introducing QuickPoll...67

Designing QuickPoll 69

    Resource Identification..69

    Resource Representation 71

    Endpoint Identification...74

    Action Identification...75

QuickPoll Architecture..78

Implementing QuickPoll 79

    Domain Implementation 82

    Repository Implementation 85

    Embedded Database.. 88

    API Implementation 88

    Summary.. 101

Chapter 5: Error Handling 103

QuickPoll Error Handling 103

Error Responses... 107

Input Field Validation... 112

Externalizing Error Messages 121

Improving RestExceptionHandler 124

Summary... 127

Chapter 6: Documenting REST Services 129

Swagger.. 130

Integrating Swagger 133

Swagger UI... 135

Customizing Swagger 136

Configuring Controllers 140

Summary... 145

Chapter 7: Versioning, Paging, and Sorting 147

Versioning 147

    Versioning Approaches... 148

    Deprecating an API 150

    QuickPoll Versioning.. 151

    SwaggerConfig 154

Pagination 157

    Page Number Pagination.. 157

    Limit Offset Pagination 158

    Cursor-Based Pagination.. 158

Time-Based Pagination 159

Pagination Data 159

QuickPoll Pagination 160

Changing Default Page Size 163

Sorting 165

Sort Ascending or Sort Descending 165

QuickPoll Sorting 166

Summary 167

Chapter 8: Security 169

Securing REST Services 169

Session-Based Security 170

HTTP Basic Authentication 171

Digest Authentication 172

Certificate-Based Security 174

XAuth 174

OAuth 2.0 176

Spring Security Overview 179

Securing QuickPoll 183

cURL 185

User Infrastructure Setup 185

UserDetailsService Implementation 189

Customizing Spring Security 191

Securing URI 192

Summary 197

Chapter 9: Clients and Testing 199

QuickPoll Java Client 199

RestTemplate 201

Getting Polls 202

Creating a Poll 205

PUT Method 206

DELETE Method 206

Handling Pagination 207

Handling Basic Authentication.. 209

Testing REST Services 211

Spring Test.. 211

Unit Testing REST Controllers 214

Integration Testing REST Controllers 220

Summary.. 222

Chapter 10: HATEOAS.. **223**

HATEOAS 224

JSON Hypermedia Types 227

JSON Hypermedia Types.. 227

HAL 228

HATEOAS in QuickPoll 230

Summary.. 236

Index.. **237**

About the Authors

Balaji Varanasi is a software development manager, author, speaker, and technology entrepreneur. He has over 14 years of experience designing and developing high-performance, scalable Java and .NET mobile applications. He has worked in the areas of security, web accessibility, search, and enterprise portals. He has a master's degree in computer science from Utah State University and serves as adjunct faculty at the University of Phoenix, teaching programming and information system courses. He has authored Apress's *Practical Spring LDAP* and has coauthored *Introducing Maven.*

Maxim Bartkov is a staff engineer with more than seven years of commercial experience in Java. Maxim specializes in building architecture for high-load systems. He is skilled in the development of distributed high-load systems, microservice architecture, Spring Framework, and system architecture. In his spare time, he writes articles for the Java community.

About the Technical Reviewer

Rohan Walia is a senior software consultant with extensive experience in client-server, web-based, and enterprise application development. He is an Oracle Certified ADF Implementation Specialist and a Sun Certified Java programmer. Rohan is responsible for designing and developing end-to-end applications consisting of various cutting-edge frameworks and utilities. His areas of expertise are Oracle ADF, Oracle WebCenter, Fusion, Spring, Hibernate, and Java/J2EE. When not working, Rohan loves to play tennis, hike, and travel. Rohan would like to thank his wife, Deepika Walia, for using all her experience and expertise to review this book.

Acknowledgments

This book would not have been possible without the support of several people, and we would like to take this opportunity to sincerely thank them.

Thanks to the amazing folks at Apress; without you, this book would not have seen the light of day. Thanks to Mark Powers for being patient and keeping us focused. Thanks to Steve Anglin for his constant support and the rest of the Apress team involved in this project.

Huge thanks to our technical reviewer Rohan Walia for his efforts and attention to detail. His valuable feedback has led to many improvements in the book.

Finally, we would like to thank our friends and family for their constant support and encouragement.

Introduction

Spring REST serves as a practical guide for designing and developing RESTful APIs using the popular Spring Framework. This book begins with a brief introduction to REST, HTTP, and web infrastructure. It then provides detailed coverage of several Spring portfolio projects such as Spring Boot, Spring MVC, Spring Data JPA, and Spring Security. The book walks through the process of designing and building a REST application while taking a deeper look into design principles and best practices for versioning, security, documentation, error handling, paging, and sorting. It also discusses techniques for building clients that consume REST services. Finally, it covers Spring MVC Test frameworks for creating unit and integration tests for REST API.

After reading the book, you will have learned

- About REST fundamentals and web infrastructure

- About Spring technologies such as Spring Boot and Spring Data JPA

- How to build REST applications with Spring technologies

- How to identify REST resources and design their representations

- Design principles for versioning REST services

- How to document REST services using Swagger

- Strategies for handling errors and communicating meaningful messages

- Techniques for handling large datasets using pagination

- Securing REST services using "Basic Auth"

- How to build REST clients using RestTemplate

- How to test REST services using the Spring MVC Test framework

How Is This Book Structured?

Chapter 1 starts with an overview of REST. We cover REST fundamentals and abstractions such as resources and representations. We then discuss web infrastructure such as URIs, HTTP methods, and HTTP response codes. We also cover Richardson's Maturity Model, which provides a classification of REST services.

Chapter 2 provides detailed coverage of Spring Web MVC. We begin with a gentle introduction to the Spring Framework and cover its two important concepts— dependency injection and aspect-oriented programming. Then we take a deeper look at the different components that make up Spring Web MVC.

Chapter 3 introduces Spring Boot, a Spring project that simplifies the bootstrapping of Spring applications. We then use Spring Boot to build a Hello World REST application. Finally, we look at some tools that can be used to access REST applications.

Chapter 4 discusses the beginnings of a RESTful application named QuickPoll. We analyze the requirements and design resources and their representations. Using Spring MVC components, we implement a set of RESTful services.

Chapter 5 covers error handling in REST services. Well-designed, meaningful error responses play an important role in the adoption of REST services. We design a custom error response for QuickPoll and implement the design. We also add validation capabilities to the inputs provided by users. Finally, we look at techniques for externalizing the error messages to property files.

Chapter 6 begins with an overview of the Swagger specification and its associated tools/frameworks. We then implement Swagger in QuickPoll to generate interactive documentation. We also customize Swagger and Swagger UI to meet our application requirements.

Chapter 7 covers the different strategies for versioning a REST API. We then look at implementing versioning in QuickPoll using the URI versioning approach. We also review the different approaches for dealing with large datasets using pagination and sorting.

Chapter 8 begins with a discussion of different strategies for securing REST services. We provide a detailed treatment of OAuth2 and review its different components. We then use the Spring Security framework to implement Basic Authentication in the QuickPoll application.

Chapter 9 covers building REST clients and testing REST APIs. We use Spring's RestTemplate features to build a REST client that works with different versions of the QuickPoll API. We then take a deeper look into the Spring MVC Test framework and examine its core classes. Finally, we write unit and integration tests to test the REST API.

Chapter 10 discusses the HATEOAS constraint that allows developers to build flexible and loosely coupled REST services. It also covers the HAL hypermedia format. We then modify the QuickPoll application such that the Poll representations are generated following HATEOAS principles.

Target Audience

Spring REST is intended for enterprise and web developers using Java and Spring who want to build REST applications. The book requires a basic knowledge of Java, Spring, and the Web but no prior exposure to REST.

Downloading the Source Code

The source code for the examples in this book can be downloaded via the **Download Source Code** button located at `www.apress.com/9781484274767`.

The downloaded source code contains a number of folders named ChapterX, in which X represents the corresponding chapter number. Each ChapterX folder contains two subfolders: a starter folder and a final folder. The starter folder houses a QuickPoll project that you can use as a basis to follow along the solution described in the corresponding chapter. Even though each chapter builds on the previous one, the starter project allows you to skip around the book. For example, if you are interested in learning about security, you can simply load the QuickPoll application under the Chapter8\starter folder and follow the solution described in Chapter 8. As the name suggests, the final folder contains the expected end state for that chapter.

Chapters 1 and 2 don't have any associated code. Therefore, the corresponding ChapterX folders for those chapters contain empty starter and final folders. In Chapter 3, we build a Hello World application, so Chapter 3's starter and final folders contain the hello-rest application. Starting from Chapter 4, the starter and final folders contain QuickPoll project source code.

Contacting the Authors

We always welcome feedback from our readers. If you have any questions or suggestions regarding the contents of this book, you can contact the authors at Balaji@inflinx.com or Maxgalayoutop@gmail.com.

CHAPTER 1

Introduction to REST

In this chapter, we will learn the following:

- REST fundamentals

- REST resources and their representations

- HTTP methods and status codes

- Richardson's Maturity Model

Today, the Web has become an integral part of our lives—from checking statuses on Facebook to ordering products online to communicating via email. The success and ubiquity of the Web have resulted in organizations applying the Web's architectural principles to building distributed applications. In this chapter, we will take a deep dive into REST, an architectural style that formalizes these principles.

What Is REST?

REST stands for REpresentational State Transfer and is an architectural style for designing distributed network applications. Roy Fielding coined the term REST in his PhD dissertation[1] and proposed the following six constraints or principles as its basis:

- Client-server—Concerns should be separated between clients and servers. This enables client and server components to evolve independently and in turn allows the system to scale.

- Stateless—The communication between client and server should be stateless. The server need not remember the state of the client. Instead, clients must include all of the necessary information in the request so that the server can understand and process it.

---

[1] `https://www.ics.uci.edu/~fielding/pubs/dissertation/top.htm`.

© Balaji Varanasi and Maxim Bartkov 2022

B. Varanasi and M. Bartkov, *Spring REST*, https://doi.org/10.1007/978-1-4842-7477-4_1

- Layered system—Multiple hierarchical layers such as gateways, firewalls, and proxies can exist between client and server. Layers can be added, modified, reordered, or removed transparently to improve scalability.

- Cache—Responses from the server must be declared as cacheable or noncacheable. This would allow the client or its intermediary components to cache responses and reuse them for later requests. This reduces the load on the server and helps improve the performance.

- Uniform Interface—All interactions between client, server, and intermediary components are based on the uniformity of their interfaces. This simplifies the overall architecture as components can evolve independently as long as they implement the agreed-on contract. The Uniform Interface constraint is further broken down into four subconstraints: resource identification, resource representations, self-descriptive messages, and Hypermedia as the Engine of Application State, or HATEOAS. We will examine some of these guiding principles in the later sections of this chapter.

- Code on demand—Clients can extend their functionality by downloading and executing code on demand. Examples include JavaScript scripts, Java applets, Silverlight, and so on. This is an optional constraint.

Applications that adhere to these constraints are considered to be RESTful. As you might have noticed, these constraints don't dictate the actual technology to be used for developing applications. Instead, adherence to these guidelines and best practices would make an application scalable, visible, portable, reliable, and able to perform better. In theory, it is possible for a RESTful application to be built using any networking infrastructure or transport protocol. In practice, RESTful applications leverage features and capabilities of the Web and use HTTP as the transport protocol.

The Uniform Interface constraint is a key feature that distinguishes REST applications from other network-based applications. Uniform Interface in a REST application is achieved through abstractions such as resources, representations, URIs, and HTTP methods. In the next sections, we will look at these important REST abstractions.

Understanding Resources

The key abstraction of information in REST is a resource.

—Roy Fielding

Fundamental to REST is the concept of resource. A resource is anything that can be accessed or manipulated. Examples of resources include "videos," "blog entries," "user profiles," "images," and even tangible things such as persons or devices. Resources are typically related to other resources. For example, in an ecommerce application, a customer can place an order for any number of products. In this scenario, the product resources are related to the corresponding order resource. It is also possible for a resource to be grouped into collections. Using the same ecommerce example, "orders" is a collection of individual "order" resources.

Identifying Resources

Before we can interact and use a resource, we must be able to identify it. The Web provides the Uniform Resource Identifier, or URI, for uniquely identifying resources. The syntax of a URI is

```
scheme:scheme-specific-part
```

The `scheme` and the `scheme-specific-part` are separated using a semicolon. Examples of a scheme include `http` or `ftp` or `mailto` and are used to define the semantics and interpretation of the rest of the URI. Take the example of the URI—`http://www.apress.com/9781484208427`. The `http` portion of the example is the scheme; it indicates that an HTTP scheme should be used for interpreting the rest of the URI. The HTTP scheme, defined as part of RFC 7230,[2] indicates that the resource identified by our example URI is located on a machine with host name `apress.com`.

Table 1-1 shows examples of URIs and the different resources they represent.

---

[2] `http://tools.ietf.org/html/rfc7230`.

Table 1-1. *URI and Resource Description*

URI	Resource description
`http://blog.example.com/posts`	Represents a collection of blog post resources.
`http://blog.example.com/posts/1`	Represents a blog post resource with identifier "1"; such resources are called singleton resources.
`http://blog.example.com/posts/1/comments`	Represents a collection of comments associated with the blog entry identified by "1"; collections such as these that reside under a resource are referred to as subcollections.
`http://blog.example.com/posts/1/comments/245`	Represents the comment resource identified by "245."

Even though a URI uniquely identifies a resource, it is possible for a resource to have more than one URI. For example, Facebook can be accessed using URIs `https://www.facebook.com` and `https://www.fb.com`. The term *URI aliases* is used to refer to such URIs that identify the same resources. URI aliases provide flexibility and added convenience such as having to type fewer characters to get to the resource.

URI Templates

When working with REST and a REST API, there will be times where you need to represent the structure of a URI rather than the URI itself. For example, in a blog application, the URI `http://blog.example.com/2014/posts` would retrieve all the blog posts created in the year 2014. Similarly, the URIs `http://blog.example.com/2013/posts`, `http://blog.example.com/2012/posts,` and so forth would return blog posts corresponding to the years 2013, 2012, and so on. In this scenario, it would be convenient for a consuming client to know the URI structure `http://blog.example.com/`**year**`/posts` that describes the range of URIs rather than individual URIs.

URI templates, defined in RFC 6570 (`http://tools.ietf.org/html/rfc6570`), provide a standardized mechanism for describing URI structure. The standardized URI template for this scenario could be

```
http://blog.example.com/{year}/posts
```

The curly braces { } indicate that the year portion of the template is a variable, often referred to as a path variable. Consuming clients can take this URI template as input, substitute the year variable with the right value, and retrieve the corresponding year's blog posts. On the server side, URL templates allow the server code to parse and retrieve the values of the variables or selected portions of URI easily.

Representation

RESTful resources are abstract entities. The data and metadata that make a RESTful resource need to be serialized into a representation before it gets sent to a client. This representation can be viewed as a *snapshot* of a resource's state at a given point in time. Consider a database table in an ecommerce application that stores information about all the available products. When an online shopper uses their browser to buy a product and requests its details, the application would provide the product details as a web page in HTML. Now, when a developer writing a native mobile application requests product details, the ecommerce application might return those details in XML or JSON format. In both scenarios, the clients didn't interact with the actual resource—the database record-holding product details. Instead, they dealt with its representation.

Note   REST components interact with a resource by transferring its representations back and forth. They never directly interact with the resource.

As noted in this product example, the same resource can have several representations. These representations can range from text-based HTML, XML, and JSON formats to binary formats such as PDFs, JPEGs, and MP4s. It is possible for the client to request a particular representation, and this process is termed as **content negotiation**. Here are the two possible content negotiation strategies:

- Postfixing the URI with the desired representation—In this strategy, a client requesting product details in JSON format would use the URI `http://www.example.com/products/143.json`. A different client might use the URI `http://www.example.com/products/143.xml` to get product details in XML format.

- Using the Accept header—Clients can populate the HTTP Accept
  header with the desired representation and send it along with the
  request. The application handling the resource would use the Accept
  header value to serialize the requested representation. The RFC 2616[3]
  provides a detailed set of rules for specifying one or more formats
  and their priorities.

Note   JSON has become the de facto standard for REST services. All of the examples in this book use JSON as the data format for requests and responses.

HTTP Methods

The "Uniform Interface" constraint restricts the interactions between client and server through a handful of standardized operations or *verbs*. On the Web, the HTTP standard[4] provides eight HTTP methods that allow clients to interact and manipulate resources. Some of the commonly used methods are GET, POST, PUT, and DELETE. Before we delve deep into HTTP methods, let's review their two important characteristics—safety and idempotency.

Note   The HTTP specification uses the term method to denote HTTP actions such as GET, PUT, and POST. However, the term HTTP verb is also used interchangeably.

Safety

A HTTP method is said to be safe if it doesn't cause any changes to the server state. Consider methods such as GET or HEAD, which are used to retrieve information/ resources from the server. These requests are typically implemented as read-only operations without causing any changes to the server's state and, hence, considered safe.

---

[3] http://www.w3.org/Protocols/rfc2616/rfc2616-sec14.html#sec14.1.
[4] https://www.ietf.org/rfc/rfc2616.txt.

Safe methods are used to retrieve resources. However, safety doesn't mean that the method must return the same value every time. For example, a GET request to retrieve Google stock might result in a different value for each call. But as long as it didn't alter any state, it is still considered safe.

In real-world implementations, there may still be side effects with a safe operation. Consider the implementation in which each request for stock prices gets logged in a database. From a purist perspective, we are changing the state of the entire system. However, from a practical standpoint, because these side effects were the sole responsibility of the server implementation, the operation is still considered to be safe.

Idempotency

An operation is considered to be idempotent if it produces the same server state whether we apply it once or any number of times. HTTP methods such as GET, HEAD (which are also safe), PUT, and DELETE are considered to be idempotent, guaranteeing that clients can repeat a request and expect the same effect as making the request once. The second and subsequent requests leave the resource state in exactly the same state as the first request did.

Consider the scenario in which you are deleting an order in an ecommerce application. On successful completion of the request, the order no longer exists on the server. Hence, any future requests to delete that order would still result in the same server state. By contrast, consider the scenario in which you are creating an order using a POST request. On successful completion of the request, a new order gets created. If you were to re-"POST" the same request, the server simply honors the request and creates a new order. Because a repeated POST request can result in unforeseen side effects, POST is not considered to be idempotent.

GET

The GET method is used to retrieve a resource's representation. For example, a GET on the URI `http://blog.example.com/posts/1` returns the representation of the blog post identified by 1. By contrast, a GET on the URI `http://blog.example.com/posts` retrieves a collection of blog posts. Because GET requests don't modify server state, they are considered to be safe and idempotent.

A hypothetical GET request to `http://blog.example.com/posts/1` and the corresponding response are shown here.

```
GET       /posts/1 HTTP/1.1
Accept:   text/html,application/xhtml+xml,application/xml;q=0.9,*/*;q=0.8
Accept-Encoding: gzip, deflate
Accept-Language: en-US,en;q=0.5
Connection: keep-alive
Host: blog.example.com
```

```
Content-Type: text/html; charset=UTF-8
Date: Sat, 10 Jan 2015 20:16:58 GMT
Server: Apache
<!DOCTYPE html PUBLIC "-//W3C//DTD XHTML 1.1//EN"
"http://www.w3.org/TR/xhtml11/DTD/xhtml11.dtd">
<html xmlns="http://www.w3.org/1999/xhtml">
    <head>
        <title>First Post</title>
    </head>
    <body>
        <h3>Hello World!!</h3>
    </body>
</html>
```

In addition to the representation, the response to GET requests includes metadata associated with the resource. This metadata is represented as a sequence of key value pairs called HTTP headers. `Content-Type` and `Server` are examples of the headers that you see in this response. Because the GET method is safe, responses to GET requests can be cached.

The simplicity of the GET method is often abused, and it is used to perform operations such as deleting or updating a resource's representation. Such usage violates standard HTTP semantics and is highly discouraged.

HEAD

On occasions, a client would like to check if a particular resource exists and doesn't really care about the actual representation. In another scenario, the client would like to know if a newer version of the resource is available before it downloads it. In both cases, a GET request could be "heavyweight" in terms of bandwidth and resources. Instead, a HEAD method is more appropriate.

The HEAD method allows a client to only retrieve the metadata associated with a resource. No resource representation gets sent to the client. This metadata represented as HTTP headers will be identical to the information sent in response to a GET request. The client uses this metadata to determine resource accessibility and recent modifications. Here is a hypothetical HEAD request and the response.

```
HEAD    /posts/1 HTTP/1.1
Accept:  text/html,application/xhtml+xml,application/xml;q=0.9,*/*;q=0.8
Accept-Encoding: gzip, deflate
Accept-Language: en-US,en;q=0.5
Connection: keep-alive
Host: blog.example.com
```

```
Connection:  Keep-Alive
Content-Type: text/html; charset=UTF-8
Date: Sat, 10 Jan 2015 20:16:58 GMT
Server: Apache
```

Like GET, the HEAD method is also safe and idempotent and responses can be cached on the client.

DELETE

The DELETE method, as the name suggests, *requests* a resource to be deleted. On receiving the request, a server deletes the resource. For resources that might take a long time to delete, the server typically sends a confirmation that it has received the request and will work on it. Depending on the service implementation, the resource may or may not be physically deleted.

On successful deletion, future GET requests on that resource would yield a "Resource Not Found" error via HTTP status code 404. We will be covering status codes in just a minute.

In this example, the client requests a post identified by 1 to be deleted. On completion, the server could return a status code 200 (OK) or 204 (No Content), indicating that the request was successfully processed.

```
Delete /posts/1  HTTP/1.1
Content-Length: 0
Content-Type: application/json
Host: blog.example.com
```

Similarly, in this example, all comments associated with post #2 get deleted.

```
Delete /posts/2/comments HTTP/1.1
Content-Length: 0
Content-Type: application/json
Host: blog.example.com
```

Because DELETE method modifies the state of the system, it is not considered to be safe. However, the DELETE method is considered idempotent; subsequent DELETE requests would still leave the resource and the system in the same state.

PUT

The PUT method allows a client to modify a resource state. A client modifies the state of a resource and sends the updated representation to the server using a PUT method. On receiving the request, the server replaces the resource's state with the new state.

In this example, we are sending a PUT request to update a post identified by 1. The request contains an updated blog post's body along with all of the other fields that make up the blog post. The server, on successful processing, would return a status code 200, indicating that the request was processed successfully.

```
PUT /posts/1     HTTP/1.1

Accept: */*
Content-Type: application/json
```

```
Content-Length: 65
Host: blog.example.com
```

BODY

```
{"title": "First Post","body": "Updated Hello World!!"}
```

Consider the case in which we just wanted to update the blog post title. The HTTP semantics dictate that as part of the PUT request, we send the full resource representation, which includes the updated title as well as other attributes such as blog post body and so on that didn't change. However, this approach would require that the client has the complete resource representation, which might not be possible if the resource is very big or has a lot of relationships. Additionally, this would require higher bandwidth for data transfers. So, for practical reasons, it is acceptable to design your API that tends to accept partial representations as part of a PUT request.

Note   To support partial updates, a new method called PATCH has been added as part of RFC 5789 (`http://www.ietf.org/rfc/rfc5789.txt`). We will be looking at the PATCH method later in this chapter.

Clients can also use PUT method to create a new resource. However, it will only be possible when the client knows the URI of the new resource. In a blogging application, for example, a client can upload an image associated with a blog post. In that scenario, the client decides the URL for the image as shown in this example:

```
PUT http://blog.example.com/posts/1/images/author.jpg
```

PUT is not a safe operation, as it changes the system state. However, it is considered idempotent, as putting the same resource once or more than once would produce the same result.

POST

The POST method is used to create resources. Typically, it is used to create resources under subcollections—resource collections that exist under a parent resource. For example, the POST method can be used to create a new blog entry in a blogging application. Here, "posts" is a subcollection of blog post resources that reside under a blog parent resource.

```
POST /posts       HTTP/1.1

Accept: */*
Content-Type: application/json
Content-Length: 63
Host: blog.example.com

BODY

{"title": "Second Post","body": "Another Blog Post."}
```

```
Content-Type: application/json
Location: posts/12345
Server: Apache
```

Unlike PUT, a POST request doesn't need to know the URI of the resource. The server is responsible for assigning an ID to the resource and deciding the URI where the resource is going to reside. In the previous example, the blogging application will process the POST request and create a new resource under http://blog.example.com/posts/12345, where "12345" is the server generated id. The Location header in the response contains the URL of the newly created resource.

The POST method is very flexible and is often used when no other HTTP method seems appropriate. Consider the scenario in which you would like to generate a thumbnail for a JPEG or PNG image. Here we ask the server to perform an action on the image binary data that we are submitting. HTTP methods such as GET and PUT don't really fit here, as we are dealing with an RPC-style operation. Such scenarios are handled using the POST method.

> **Note**   The term "controller resource" has been used to describe executable resources that take inputs, perform some action, and return outputs. Although these types of resources don't fit the true REST resource definition, they are very convenient to expose complex operations.

The POST method is not considered safe, as it changes system state. Also, multiple POST invocations would result in multiple resources being generated, making it nonidempotent.

PATCH

As we discussed earlier, the HTTP specification requires the client to send the entire resource representation as part of a PUT request. The PATCH method proposed as part of RFC 5789 (`http://tools.ietf.org/html/rfc5789`) is used to perform partial resource updates. It is neither safe nor idempotent. Here is an example that uses PATCH method to update a blog post title.

PATCH /posts/1   HTTP/1.1

```
Accept: */*
Content-Type: application/json
Content-Length: 59
Host: blog.example.com

BODY

{"replace": "title","value": "New Awesome title"}
```

The request body contains a description of changes that need to be performed on the resource. In the example, the request body uses the `"replace"` command to indicate that the value of the `"title"` field needs to be replaced.

There is no standardized format for describing the changes to the server as part of a PATCH request. A different implementation might use the following format to describe the same change:

```
{"change" : "name", "from" : "Post Title", "to" : "New Awesome Title"}
```

Currently, there is a work in progress (`http://tools.ietf.org/html/draft-ietf-appsawg-json-patch`) for defining a PATCH format for JSON. This lack of standard has resulted in implementations that describe change sets in a simpler format, as shown here:

```
{"name" : "New Awesome Title"}
```

CRUD AND HTTP VERBS

Data-driven applications typically use the term CRUD to indicate four basic persistence functions—Create, Read, Update, and Delete. Some developers building REST applications have mistakenly associated the four popular HTTP verbs GET, POST, PUT, and DELETE with CRUD semantics. The typical association often seen is

```
Create -> POST
Update -> PUT
Read -> GET
Delete -> DELETE
```

These correlations are true for Read and Delete operations. However, it is not as straightforward for Create/Update and POST/PUT. As you have seen earlier in this chapter, PUT can be used to create a resource as long as idempotency constraint is met. In the same way, it was never considered non-RESTful if POST is used for update (`http://roy.gbiv.com/untangled/2009/it-is-okay-to-use-post`). It is also possible for a client to use PATCH for updating a resource.

Therefore, it is important for API designers to use the right verbs for a given operation than simply using a 1-1 mapping with CRUD.

HTTP Status Codes

The HTTP status codes allow a server to communicate the results of processing a client's request. These status codes are grouped into the following categories:

- Informational codes—Status codes indicating that the server has received the request but hasn't completed processing it. These intermediate response codes are in the 100 series.

- Success codes—Status codes indicating that the request has been successfully received and processed. These codes are in the 200 series.

- Redirection codes—Status codes indicating that the request has been processed but the client must perform an additional action to complete the request. These actions typically involve redirecting to a different location to get the resource. These codes are in the 300 series.

- Client error codes—Status codes indicating that there was an error or a problem with client's request. These codes are in the 400 series.

- Server error codes—Status codes indicating that there was an error on the server while processing the client's request. These codes are in the 500 series.

The HTTP status codes play an important role in REST API design as meaningful codes help communicate the right status, enabling the client to react appropriately. Table 1-2 shows some of the important status codes into which you typically run.

Table 1-2. *HTTP status codes and their descriptions*

Status code	Description
100 (Continue)	Indicates that the server has received the first part of the request and the rest of the request should be sent.
200 (OK)	Indicates that all went well with the request.
201 (Created)	Indicates that request was completed and a new resource got created.
202 (Accepted)	Indicates that request has been accepted but is still being processed.
204 (No Content)	Indicates that the server has completed the request and has no entity body to send to the client.
301 (Moved Permanently)	Indicates that the requested resource has been moved to a new location and a new URI needs to be used to access the resource.
400 (Bad Request)	Indicates that the request is malformed and the server is not able to understand the request.

(continued)

Table 1-2. (*continued*)

Status code	Description
401 (Unauthorized)	Indicates that the client needs to authenticate before accessing the resource. If the request already contains client's credentials, then a 401 indicates invalid credentials (e.g., bad password).
403 (Forbidden)	Indicates that the server understood the request but is refusing to fulfill it. This could be because the resource is being accessed from a blacklisted IP address or outside the approved time window.
404 (Not Found)	Indicates that the resource at the requested URI doesn't exist.
406 (Not Acceptable)	Indicates that the server is capable of processing the request; however, the generated response may not be acceptable to the client. This happens when the client becomes too picky with its accept headers.
500 (Internal Server Error)	Indicates that there was an error on the server while processing the request and that the request can't be completed.
503 (Service Unavailable)	Indicates that the request can't be completed, as the server is overloaded or going through scheduled maintenance.

Richardson's Maturity Model

The Richardson's Maturity Model (RMM), developed by Leonard Richardson, classifies REST-based web services on how well they adhere to REST principles. Figure 1-1 shows the four levels of this classification.

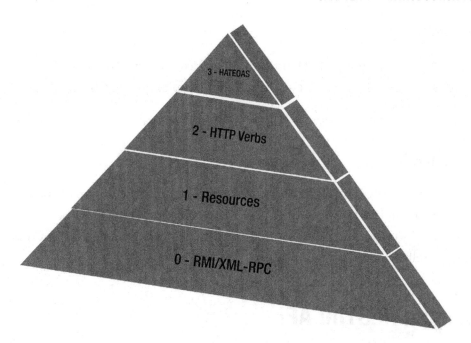

Figure 1-1. *RMM levels*

RMM can be valuable in understanding the different styles of web service and their designs, benefits, and trade-offs.

Level Zero

This is the most rudimentary maturity level for a service. Services in this level use HTTP as the transport mechanism and perform remote procedure calls on a single URI. Typically, POST or GET HTTP methods are employed for service calls. SOAP- and XML-RPC-based web services fall under this level.

Level One

The next level adheres to the REST principles more closely and introduces multiple URIs, one per resource. Complex functionality of a large service endpoint is broken down into multiple resources. However, services in this layer use one HTTP verb, typically POST, to perform all of the operations.

Level Two

Services in this level leverage HTTP protocol and make the right use of HTTP verbs and status codes available in the protocol. Web services implementing CRUD operations are good examples of level two services.

Level Three

This is the most mature level for a service and is built around the notion of Hypermedia as the Engine of Application State, or HATEOAS. Services in this level allow discoverability by providing responses that contain links to other related resources and controls that tell the client what to do next.

Building a RESTful API

Designing and implementing a beautiful RESTful API is no less than an art. It takes time, effort, and several iterations. A well-designed RESTful API allows your end users to consume the API easily and makes its adoption easier. At a high level, here are the steps involved in building a RESTful API:

1. Identify resources—Central to REST are resources. We start modeling different resources that are of interest to our consumers. Often, these resources can be the application's domain or entities. However, a one-to-one mapping is not always required.

2. Identify endpoints—The next step is to design URIs that map resources to endpoints. In Chapter 4, we will look at best practices for designing and naming endpoints.

3. Identify actions—Identify the HTTP methods that can be used to perform operations on the resources.

4. Identify responses—Identify the supported resource representation for the request and response along with the right status codes to be returned.

In the rest of the book, we will look at best practices for designing a RESTful API and implementing it using Spring technologies.

Summary

REST has become the de facto standard for building services today. In this chapter, we covered the fundamentals of REST and abstractions such as resources, representations, URIs, and HTTP methods that make up REST's Uniform Interface. We also looked at RMM, which provides a classification of REST services.

In the next chapter, we will take a deep dive into Spring and its related technologies that simplify REST service development.

CHAPTER 2

Spring Web MVC Primer

In this chapter, we will discuss the following:

- Spring and its features
- The Model View Controller pattern
- Spring Web MVC and its components

The Java ecosystem is filled with frameworks such as Jersey and RESTEasy, which allow you to develop REST applications. Spring Web MVC is one such popular web framework that simplifies web and REST application development. We begin this chapter with an overview of the Spring Framework and take a deep dive into Spring Web MVC and its components.

Note This book doesn't give a comprehensive overview of Spring and Spring Web MVC. Refer to *Pro Spring* and *Pro Spring MVC and WebFlux* (both published by Apress) for detailed treatment of these concepts.

Spring Overview

The Spring Framework has become the de facto standard for building Java/Java EE-based enterprise applications. Originally written by Rod Johnson in 2002, the Spring Framework is one of the suites of projects owned and maintained by Pivotal Software Inc. (`http://spring.io`). Among many other things, the Spring Framework provides a dependency injection model[1] that reduces plumbing code for application development, supports aspect-oriented programming (AOP) for implementing crosscutting concerns,

---

[1] `http://martinfowler.com/articles/injection.html.`

© Balaji Varanasi and Maxim Bartkov 2022
B. Varanasi and M. Bartkov, *Spring REST*, https://doi.org/10.1007/978-1-4842-7477-4_2

and makes it easy to integrate with other frameworks and technologies. The Spring
Framework is made up of different modules that offer services such as data access,
instrumentation, messaging, testing, and web integration. The different Spring
Framework modules and their groupings are shown in Figure 2-1.

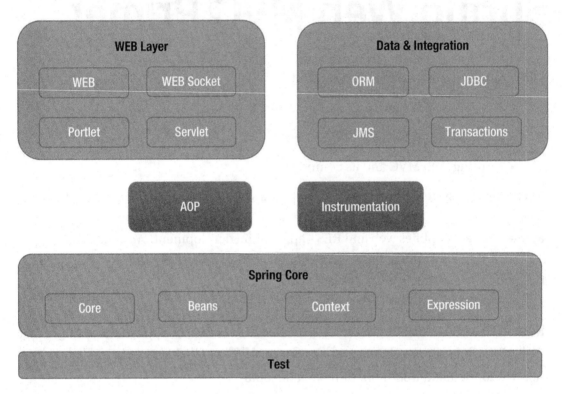

Figure 2-1. *Spring Framework modules*

As a developer, you are not forced to use everything that the Spring Framework has
to offer. The modularity of the Spring Framework allows you to pick and choose the
modules based on your application needs. In this book, we will be focusing on the web
module for developing REST services. Additionally, we will be using a few other Spring
portfolio projects such as Spring Data, Spring Security, and Spring Boot. These projects
are built on top of the infrastructure provided by the Spring Framework modules and are
intended to simplify data access, authentication/authorization, and Spring application
creation.

Developing Spring-based applications requires a thorough understanding of two
core concepts—dependency injection and aspect-oriented programming.

Dependency Injection

At the heart of the Spring Framework lies dependency injection (DI). As the name suggests, dependency injection allows dependencies to be *injected* into components that need them. This relieves those components from having to create or locate their dependencies, allowing them to be loosely coupled.

To better understand DI, consider the scenario of purchasing a product in an online retail store. Completing a purchase is typically implemented using a component such as an OrderService. The OrderService itself would interact with an OrderRepository that would create order details in a database and a NotificationComponent that would send out the order confirmation to the customer. In a traditional implementation, the OrderService creates (typically in its constructor) instances of OrderRepository and NotificationComponent and uses them. Even though there is nothing wrong with this approach, it can lead to hard-to-maintain, hard-to-test, and highly coupled code.

DI, by contrast, allows us to take a different approach when dealing with dependencies. With DI, you let an external process such as Spring create dependencies, manage dependencies, and inject those dependencies into the objects that need them. So, with DI, Spring would create the OrderRepository and NotificationComponent and then hand over those dependencies to the OrderService. This decouples OrderService from having to deal with OrderRepository/NotificationComponent creation, making it easier to test. It allows each component to evolve independently, making development and maintenance easier. Also, it makes it easier to swap these dependencies with different implementations or use these components in a different context.

Aspect-Oriented Programming

Aspect-oriented programming (AOP) is a programming model that implements crosscutting logic or concerns. Logging, transactions, metrics, and security are some examples of concerns that span (crosscut) different parts of an application. These concerns don't deal with business logic and are often duplicated across the application. AOP provides a standardized mechanism called an *aspect* for encapsulating such concerns in a single location. The aspects are then *weaved* into other objects so that the crosscutting logic is automatically applied across the entire application.

Spring provides a pure Java-based AOP implementation through its Spring AOP module. Spring AOP does not require any special compilation nor changes to the class loader hierarchy. Instead, Spring AOP uses proxies for weaving aspects into Spring beans

23

at runtime. Figure 2-2 provides a representation of this behavior. When a method on the target bean gets called, the proxy intercepts the call. It then applies the aspect logic and invokes the target bean method.

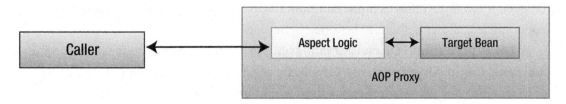

Figure 2-2. *Spring AOP proxy*

Spring provides two-proxy implementations—JDK dynamic proxy and CGLIB proxy. If the target bean implements an interface, Spring will use JDK dynamic proxy to create the AOP proxy. If the class doesn't implement an interface, Spring uses CGLIB to create a proxy.

You can read more about JDK dynamic proxy in the official documentation: `https://docs.oracle.com/javase/8/docs/technotes/guides/reflection/proxy.html`

Spring Web MVC Overview

Spring Web MVC, part of the Spring Framework's web module, is a popular technology for building web-based applications. It is based on the model-view-controller architecture and provides a rich set of annotations and components. Over the years, the framework has evolved; it currently provides a rich set of configuration annotations and features such as flexible view resolution and powerful data binding.

Model View Controller Pattern

The Model View Controller, or MVC, is an architectural pattern for building decoupled web applications. This pattern decomposes the UI layer into the following three components:

> Model—The model represents data or state. In a web-based banking application, information representing accounts, transactions, and statements are examples of the model.

View—Provides a visual representation of the model. This is what the user interacts with by providing inputs and viewing the output. In our banking application, web pages showing accounts and transactions are examples of views.

Controller—The controller is responsible for handling user actions such as button clicks. It then interacts with services or repositories to prepare the model and hands the prepared model over to an appropriate view.

Each component has specific responsibility. The interaction between them is shown in Figure 2-3. The interaction begins with the Controller preparing the model and selecting an appropriate view to be rendered. The View uses the data from the model for rendering. Further interactions with the View are sent to the Controller, which starts the process all over again.

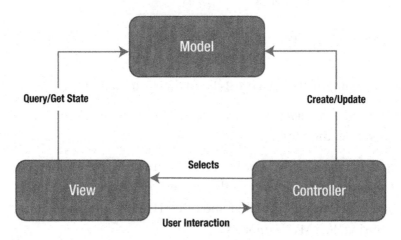

Figure 2-3. *Model View Controller interaction*

Spring Web MVC Architecture

Spring's Web MVC implementation revolves around the DispatcherServlet—an implementation of the FrontController Pattern[2] that acts as an entry point for handling requests. Spring Web MVC's architecture is shown in Figure 2-4.

---

[2] http://www.oracle.com/technetwork/java/frontcontroller-135648.html.

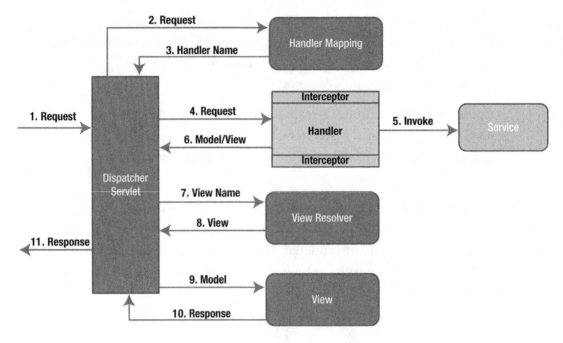

Figure 2-4. *Spring Web MVC's architecture*

The different components in Figure 2-4 and their interactions include the following:

1. The interaction begins with the DispatcherServlet receiving the request from the client.

2. DispatcherServlet queries one or more HandlerMapping to figure out a Handler that can service the request. A Handler is a generic way of addressing a Controller and other HTTP-based endpoints that Spring Web MVC supports.

3. The HandlerMapping component uses the request path to determine the right Handler and passes it to the DispatcherServlet. The HandlerMapping also determines a list of Interceptors that need to get executed before (Pre-) and after (Post-) Handler execution.

4. The DispatcherServlet then executes the Pre-Process Interceptors if any are appropriate and passes the control to the Handler.

5. The Handler interacts with any Service(s) needed and prepares the model.

6. The Handler also determines the name of the view that needs to get rendered in the output and sends it to DispatcherServlet. The Post-Process Interceptors then get executed.

7. This is followed by the DispatcherServlet passing the logical view name to a ViewResolver, which determines and passes the actual View implementation.

8. The DispatcherServlet then passes the control and model to the View, which generates response. This ViewResolver and View abstraction allow the DispatcherServlet to be decoupled from a particular View implementation.

9. The DispatcherServlet returns the generated response over to the client.

Spring Web MVC Components

In the previous section, you were introduced to Spring Web MVC components such as HandlerMapping and ViewResolver. In this section, we will take a deeper look at those as well as additional Spring Web MVC components.

Note   In this book, we will be using Java configuration for creating Spring beans. Contrary to XML-based configuration, Java configuration provides compile-time safety, flexibility, and added power/control.

Controller

Controllers in Spring Web MVC are declared using the stereotype `org. springframework.stereotype.Controller`. A stereotype in Spring designates roles or responsibilities of a class or an interface. Listing 2-1 shows a basic controller.

Listing 2-1. HomeController Implementation

```
@Controller
public class HomeController {
        @GetMapping("/home.html")
        public String showHomePage() {
                return "home";
        }
}
```

The @Controller annotation designates the HomeController class as a MVC controller. The @GetMapping is a composed annotation that acts as a shortcut for @ RequestMapping(method = RequestMethod.GET). @GetMapping annotation maps web requests to handler classes and handler methods. In this case, the @GetMapping indicates that when a request for home.html is made, the showHomePage method should get executed. The showHomePage method has a tiny implementation and simply returns the logical view name home. This controller did not prepare any model in this example.

Model

Spring provides the org.springframework.ui.Model interface that serves as holder for model attributes. Listing 2-2 shows the Model interface with the available methods. As the names suggest, the addAttribute and addAttributes methods can be used to add attributes to the model object.

Listing 2-2. Model Interface

```
public interface Model {

        Model addAttribute(String attributeName, Object attributeValue);

        Model addAttribute(Object attributeValue);

        Model addAllAttributes(Collection<?> attributeValues);

        Model addAllAttributes(Map<String, ?> attributes);

        Model mergeAttributes(Map<String, ?> attributes);
```

```
    boolean containsAttribute(String attributeName);

    Map<String, Object> asMap();

    Object getAttribute(String attributeName);

}
```

The easiest way for a controller to work with a model object is by declaring it as a method parameter. Listing 2-3 shows the showHomePage method with the Model parameter. In the method implementation, we are adding the currentDate attribute to the model object.

Listing 2-3. showHomePage with Model Attribute

```
@GetMapping("/home.html")
public String showHomePage(Model model) {
        model.addAttribute("currentDate", new Date());
        return "home";
}
```

The Spring Framework strives to decouple our applications from the framework's classes. So, a popular approach for working with model objects is to use a java.util. Map instance as shown in Listing 2-4. Spring would use the passed-in Map parameter instance to enrich the model that gets exposed to the view.

Listing 2-4. showHomePage with Map Attribute

```
@GetMapping("/home.html")
public String showHomePage(Map model) {
        model.put("currentDate", new Date());
        return "home";
}
```

View

Spring Web MVC supports a variety of view technologies such as JSP, Velocity, FreeMarker, and XSLT. Spring Web MVC uses the org.springframework.web.servlet. View interface to accomplish this. The View interface has two methods, as shown in Listing 2-5.

Listing 2-5. View Interface API

```
public interface View
{
        String getContentType();

        void render(Map<String, ?> model, HttpServletRequest request,
        HttpServletResponse response) throws Exception;
}
```

Concrete implementations of the View interface are responsible for rendering the response. This is accomplished by overriding the render method. The getContentType method returns the generated view's content type. Table 2-1 shows important View implementations that Spring Web MVC provides out of the box. You will notice that all of these implementations reside inside the org.springframework.web.servlet.view package.

Table 2-1. *Spring Web MVC View Implementations*

Class name	Description
org.springframework.web.servlet.view. json.MappingJackson2JsonView	View implementation that encodes model attributes and returns JSON
org.springframework.web.servlet.view. xslt.XsltView	View implementation that performs XSLT transformation and returns the response
org.springframework.web.servlet.view. InternalResourceView	View implementation that delegates the request to a JSP page inside the web application
org.springframework.web.servlet.view. tiles2.TilesView	View implementation that uses Apache Tiles configuration for Tile definition and rendering
org.springframework.web.servlet.view. JstlView	Specialized implementation of InternalResourceView that supports JSP pages using JSTL
org.springframework.web.servlet.view. RedirectView	View implementation that redirects to a different (absolute or relative) URL

Listing 2-6 shows the reimplementation of the HomeController that we looked at earlier. Here we are creating an instance of JstlView and setting the JSP page that we need to be rendered.

Listing 2-6. HomeController View Implementation

```
@Controller
public class HomeController {
        @RequestMapping("/home.html")
        public View showHomePage() {
                JstlView view = new JstlView();
                view.setUrl("/WEB-INF/pages/home.jsp");
                return view;
        }
}
```

Controller implementations typically don't deal with view instances. Instead, they return logical view names, as shown in Listing 2-1, and let view resolvers determine and create view instances. This decouples the controllers from tying to a specific view implementation and makes it easy to swap view implementations. Also, the controllers no longer need to know intricacies such as the location of the views.

@RequestParam

The @RequestParam annotation is used to bind Servlet request parameters to handler/ controller method parameters. The request parameter values are automatically converted to the specified method parameter type using type conversion. Listing 2-7 shows two usages of @RequestParam. In the first usage, Spring looks for a request parameter named query and maps its value to the method parameter query. In the second usage, Spring looks for a request parameter named page, converts its value to an integer, and maps it to the pageNumber method parameter.

Listing 2-7. RequestParam Usage

```
@GetMapping("/search.html")
public String search(@RequestParam String query, @RequestParam("page") int
pageNumber) {
        model.put("currentDate", new Date());
        return "home";
}
```

When a method parameter is annotated using @RequestParam, the specified request parameter must be available in the client request. If the parameter is missing, Spring will throw a MissingServletRequestParameterException exception. One way to address this is to set the required attribute to false, as shown in Listing 2-8. The other option is to use the defaultValue attribute to specify a default value.

Listing 2-8. Making a Request Parameter Not Required

```
@GetMapping("/search.html")
public String search(@RequestParam String query,
@RequestParam(value="page", required=false) int pageNumber,
@RequestParam(value="size", defaultValue="10") int pageSize) {
        model.put("currentDate", new Date());
        return "home";
}
```

@RequestMapping

As we learned in the "Controller" section, the @RequestMapping annotation is used to map a web request to a handler class or handler method. @RequestMapping provides several attributes that can be used to narrow down these mappings. Table 2-2 shows the different elements along with their descriptions.

Table 2-2. *RequestMapping Elements*

Element name	Description
Method	Restricts a mapping to a specific HTTP method such as GET, POST, HEAD, OPTIONS, PUT, PATCH, DELETE, TRACE
Produces	Narrows mapping to media type that is produced by the method
Consumes	Narrows mapping to media type that the method consumes
Headers	Narrows mapping to the headers that should be present
Name	Allows you to assign a name to the mapping
Params	Restricts a mapping to the supplied parameter name and value
Value	Narrowing path for a specific handler method (if don't have any elements, by default value is the main element)
Path	Narrowing path for a specific handler method (alias for value)

The default HTTP method mapped by @RequestMapping is GET. This behavior can be changed using the method element shown in Listing 2-9. Spring invokes the saveUser method only when a POST operation is performed. A GET request on saveUser will result in an exception thrown. Spring provides a handy RequestMethod enumeration with the list of HTTP methods available.

Listing 2-9. POST Method Example

```
@RequestMapping(value="/saveuser.html", method=RequestMethod.POST)
public String saveUser(@RequestParam String username, @RequestParam String
password) {
        // Save User logic
        return "success";
}
```

@RequestMapping Shortcut Annotations

You can use "shortcut annotation" for @RequestMapping.

It looks more readable because you can use "shortcut annotation" instead of @RequestMapping.

All shortcut annotations inherit all elements from @RequestMapping, without method, because the method is already in the title of the annotation.

For example, @GetMapping is exactly the same as @RequestMapping(method = RequestMethod.GET).

Table 2-3. *Shortcut Annotations for @RequestMapping*

Annotation	Replacement
@GetMapping	@RequestMapping(method = RequestMethod.GET)
@PostMapping	@RequestMapping(method = RequestMethod.POST)
@PutMapping	@RequestMapping(method = RequestMethod.PUT)
@DeleteMapping	@RequestMapping(method = RequestMethod.DELETE)
@PatchMapping	@RequestMapping(method = RequestMethod.PATCH)

The produces element indicates the media type, such as JSON or XML or HTML, produced by the mapped method. The produces element can take a single media type or multiple media types as its value. Listing 2-10 shows the search method with the produces element added. The MediaType.TEXT_HTML value indicates that when a GET request is performed on search.html, the method returns an HTML response.

Listing 2-10. Produces Element Example

```
@GetMapping(value="/search.html", produces="MediaType.TEXT_HTML")
public String search(@RequestParam String query,
@RequestParam(value="page", required=false) int pageNumber) {
        model.put("currentDate", new Date());
        return "home";
}
```

It is possible for the client to perform a GET request on /search.html but send an Accept header with value application/JSON. In that scenario, Spring will not invoke the search method. Instead, it will return a 404 error. The produces element provides a convenient way to restrict mappings to content types that the controller can serve. In the same fashion, the consumes element is used to indicate the media type that the annotated method consumes.

ACCEPT AND CONTENT-TYPE HEADER

As discussed in Chapter 1, REST resources can have multiple representations. REST clients typically use the `Accept` and `Content-Type` headers to work with these representations.

REST clients use the `Accept` header to indicate the representations that they accept. The HTTP specification allows a client to send a prioritized list of different media types that it will accept as responses. On receiving the request, the server will send the representation with the highest priority. To understand this, consider the default `Accept` header for Firefox browser:

`text/html,application/xhtml+xml,application/xml;q=0.9,*/*;q=0.8`

The q parameter, also known as relative quality parameter, indicates the degree of preference and has values ranging from 0 to 1. From the string, we can infer that the HTML and XHTML will have a priority of 1 because they don't have an associated q value. The XML media type has priority 0.9, and the rest of the representations have a priority of 0.8. On receiving this request, the server would try to send an HTML/XHTML representation because it has the highest priority.

In a similar fashion, REST clients use the `Content-Type` header to indicate the media type of the request being sent to the server. This allows the server to properly interpret the request and parse the contents correctly. If the server is unable to parse the content, it will send a 415 Unsupported Media Type error status code.

Spring Web MVC allows flexible signatures for methods annotated with `@RequestMapping`. This includes variable method parameters and method return types. Table 2-4 lists the important arguments allowed. For a detailed list of allowed arguments, refer to Spring's Javadocs at `http://docs.spring.io/spring/docs/current/javadoc-api/org/springframework/web/bind/annotation/RequestMapping.html`.

Table 2-4. *Method Arguments and Descriptions*

Method argument	Description
HttpServletRequest/ HttpServletResponse	HTTP Servlet request and response objects. Allows raw access to client's data, such as request parameters and headers.
HttpSession	Instance representing a user's HTTP session.
Command object	A POJO or model object that Spring populates/binds with the user-submitted data. The command object can be annotated with @ModelAttribute.
BindingResult	Instance representing a command object's validation and binding. This parameter must immediately precede the command object.
HttpEntity<?>	Instance representing an HTTP request. Each HttpEntity is composed of request body and a set of headers.
Principal	A java.security.Principal instance that represents the authenticated user.

The different return types supported in methods annotated with @RequestMapping are shown in Table 2-5.

Table 2-5. *Return Types and Descriptions*

Return type	Description
String	Represents the logical view name. Registered view resolvers are employed to resolve the physical view, and a response is generated.
View	Instance representing a view. In this case, no view resolution is performed and the view object is responsible for generating the response. Examples include JstlView, VelocityView, RedirectView, and so on.
HttpEntity<?>	Instance representing an HTTP response. Each HttpEntity is composed of response body and a set of headers.
HttpHeaders	Instance capturing the headers to be returned. Response will have an empty body.
Pojo	Java object that is considered to be a model attribute. A specialized RequestToViewNameTranslator is used to determine the appropriate logical view name.

Path Variables

The @RequestMapping annotation supports dynamic URIs via URI templates. As discussed in Chapter 1, URI templates are URIs with placeholders or variables. The @PathVariable annotation allows you to access and use these placeholders via method parameters. Listing 2-11 gives an example of @PathVariable. In this scenario, the getUser method is designed to serve user information associated with the path variable {username}. The client would perform a GET on the URL /users/jdoe to retrieve user information associated with username jdoe.

Listing 2-11. PathVariable Example

```
@RequestMapping("/users/{username}")
public User getUser(@PathVariable("username") String username) {
        User user = null;
        // Code to construct user object using username
        return user;
}
```

View Resolver

As discussed in the previous sections, a Spring Web MVC controller can return an org.springframework.web.servlet.View instance or a logical view name. When a logical view name is returned, a ViewResolver is employed to resolve the view to a View implementation. If this process fails for some reason, a javax.servlet.ServletException is thrown. The ViewResolver interface has a single method and is shown in Listing 2-12.

Listing 2-12. ViewResolver Interface

```
public interface ViewResolver
{
        View resolveViewName(String viewName, Locale locale) throws
        Exception;
}
```

Table 2-6 lists some of the `ViewResolver` implementations provided by Spring Web MVC.

As you might have noticed, the different view resolvers in Table 2-6 mimic the different types of views we looked at earlier. Listing 2-13 shows the code required for creating an `InternalViewResolver`.

Also Listing 2-13 shows @Bean annotation—in short, all methods defined by @Bean in a class annotated by @Configuration will return objects, which is controlled by Spring Framework, and with help we can define behavior for some objects and call the object everywhere using @Inject or @Autowired annotation if it is needed. Every object created by Spring Framework will be defined as a @Bean by default.

Table 2-6. *ViewResolver Implementations and Descriptions*

Return type	Description
BeanNameViewResolver	ViewResolver implementation that looks for a bean with an id that matches the logical view name in the ApplicationContext. If it doesn't find the bean in the ApplicationContext, a null is returned.
InternalResourceViewResolver	ViewResolver that looks for an internal resource that has the logical view name. The location of the internal resource is typically computed by prefixing and suffixing the logical name with path and extension information.
ContentNegotiatingViewResolver	ViewResolver that delegates the view resolution to other view resolvers. The choice of the view resolver is based on the requested media type, which itself is determined using an Accept header or file extension or URL parameter.
TilesViewResolver	ViewResolver that looks for a template in the Tiles configuration that matches the logical view name.

Listing 2-13. InternalViewResolver Example

```
@Bean
public ViewResolver viewResolver() {
    InternalResourceViewResolver viewResolver = new
    InternalResourceViewResolver();
    viewResolver.setPrefix("/WEB-INF/jsp/");
    viewResolver.setSuffix(".jsp");
    return viewResolver;
}
```

Exception Handler

Exceptions are part of any application, and Spring provides the HandlerException Resolver mechanism for handling those unexpected exceptions. The HandlerException Resolver abstraction is similar to the ViewResolver and is used to resolve exceptions to error views. Listing 2-14 shows the HandlerExceptionResolver API.

Listing 2-14. HandlerExceptionResolver API

```
public interface HandlerExceptionResolver {
ModelAndView resolveException(HttpServletRequest request,
HttpServletResponse response,
Object handler, Exception ex);
}
```

Spring provides several out-of-the-box implementations of HandlerExceptionResolver, as shown in Table 2-7.

Table 2-7. *HandlerExceptionResolver Implementations and Descriptions*

Resolver implementation	Description
org.springframework.web.servlet.handler.SimpleMappingExceptionResolver	Exception resolver implementation that maps exception class names to view names.
org.springframework.web.servlet.mvc.support.DefaultHandlerExceptionResolver	Exception resolver implementation that translates standard Spring exceptions to HTTP status codes.
org.springframework.web.servlet.mvc.annotation.ResponseStatusExceptionResolver	Custom exceptions in Spring applications can be annotated with @ResponseStatus, which takes a HTTP status code as its value. This exception resolver translates the exceptions to its mapped HTTP status codes.
org.springframework.web.servlet.mvc.method.annotation.ExceptionHandlerExceptionResolver	Exception resolver implementation that resolves exceptions using annotated @ExceptionHandler methods.

The SimpleMappingExceptionResolver has been around for a really long time. Spring 3 introduced a new way of handling exceptions using the @ExceptionHandler strategy. This provides a mechanism for handling errors in REST-based services where there is really no view to show but, rather, return data. Listing 2-15 shows a controller with an exception handler. Any methods that now throw a SQLException in the HomeController will get handled in the handleSQLException method. The handleSQLException simply creates a ResponseEntity instance and returns it. However, additional operations such as logging, returning additional diagnostic data, and so on can be performed.

Listing 2-15. ExceptionHandler Example

```
@Controller
public class HomeController {
        @ExceptionHandler(SQLException.class)
        public ResponseEntity handleSQLException() {
```

```
ResponseEntity responseEntity = new ResponseEntity(HttpStatus.INTERNAL_
SERVER_ERROR);
                return responseEntity;
    }

    @GetMapping("/stream")
    public void streamMovie(HttpServletResponse response) throws
    SQLException {

    }
}
```

The @ExceptionHandler annotated methods can only handle exceptions that occur in the controller or its subclasses. So, if we need to handle SQL exceptions in other controllers, then we need to copy and paste the handleSQLException method in all of those controllers. This approach can pose severe limitations, as exception handling is truly a crosscutting concern and should be centralized.

To address this, Spring provides the @ControllerAdvice annotation. Methods in classes annotated with @ControllerAdvice get applied to all the @ RequestMapping methods. Listing 2-16 shows the GlobalExceptionHandler with the handleSQLException method. As you can see, the GlobalExceptionHandler extends Spring's ResponseEntityExceptionHandler, which converts default Spring Web MVC exceptions to a ResponseEntity with HTTP status codes.

Listing 2-16. GlobalExceptionHandler Example

```
@ControllerAdvice
public class GlobalExceptionHandler extends ResponseEntityExceptionHandler
{

    @ExceptionHandler(SQLException.class)
    public ResponseEntity handleSQLException() {
ResponseEntity responseEntity = new ResponseEntity(HttpStatus.INTERNAL_
SERVER_ERROR);
                return responseEntity;
    }
}
```

Interceptors

Spring Web MVC provides the notion of interceptors to implement concerns that crosscut across different handlers. Consider the scenario in which you want to prevent unauthenticated access to a set of controllers. An interceptor allows you to centralize this access logic without you having to copy and paste the code in every controller. As the name suggests, interceptors intercept a request; they do so at the following three points:

- Before the controller gets executed. This allows the interceptor to decide if it needs to continue the execution chain or return with an exception or custom response.

- After the controller gets executed but before the response is sent out. This allows the interceptor to provide any additional model objects to the view.

- After the response is sent out allowing any resource cleanup.

Note   Spring Web MVC interceptors are similar to HTTP servlet filters. Both can be used to intercept a request and execute common concerns. However, there are a few differences between them that are worth noting. Filters have the capability to wrap or even swap the `HttpServletRequest` and `HttpServletResponse` objects. Interceptors can't decorate or swap those objects. Interceptors are Spring-managed beans, and we can easily inject other spring beans in them. Filters are container-managed instances; they don't provide a straightforward mechanism for injecting Spring-managed beans.

Spring Web MVC provides the `HandlerInterceptor` interface for implementing interceptors. Listing 2-17 gives the `HandlerInterceptor` interface. As you can see, the three methods correspond to the three interceptor features that we just discussed.

Listing 2-17. HandlerInterceptor API

```
public interface HandlerInterceptor{
    void afterCompletion(HttpServletRequest request, HttpServletResponse
    response, Object handler, Exception ex);
    void postHandle(HttpServletRequest request, HttpServletResponse
    response, Object handler, ModelAndView modelAndView);
    boolean preHandle(HttpServletRequest request, HttpServletResponse
    response, Object handler);
}
```

Listing 2-18 gives a simple interceptor implementation. As you can see, the SimpleInterceptor class extends HandlerInterceptorAdapter. The HandlerInterceptorAdapter is a convenient abstract class that implements the HandlerInterceptor interface and provides default implementations of its methods.

Listing 2-18. Spring Web MVC Interceptor Example

```
public class SimpleInterceptor extends HandlerInterceptorAdapter {
        private static final Logger logger = Logger.
        getLogger(SimpleInterceptor.class);

public boolean preHandle(HttpServletRequest request, HttpServletResponse
response, Object handler) throws Exception {
        logger.info("Inside the prehandle");

        return false;
    }
}
```

Interceptors can be registered in a Spring Web application using the InterceptorRegistry strategy. When using Java configuration, this is typically achieved by creating a configuration class that extends WebMvcConfigurerAdapter. Spring Web MVC's WebMvcConfigurerAdapter class provides the addInterceptors method that can be used to access the InterceptorRegistry. Listing 2-19 shows the code registering two interceptors: LocalInterceptor that comes out of the box with Spring and our SimpleInterceptor.

Listing 2-19. Example Registering Interceptors

```
@Configuration
@EnableWebMvc
@ComponentScan(basePackages = { "com.apress.springrest.web" })
public class WebConfig extends WebMvcConfigurerAdapter {

    @Override
    public void addInterceptors(InterceptorRegistry registry) {
        registry.addInterceptor(new LocaleChangeInterceptor());
        registry.addInterceptor(new SimpleInterceptor()).addPathPatterns
        ("/auth/**");
    }
}
```

When an interceptor is added to the interceptor registry, the interceptor gets applied to all of the handler mappings. So, the `LocaleChangeInterceptor` in Listing 2-19 gets applied to all the handler mappings. However, it is also possible to restrict the interceptor to certain URLs. This is demonstrated in Listing 2-19 using the `addPathPatterns` method. Here we are indicating that the `SimpleInterceptor` should be applied to only the URLs that are under the `auth` path.

Summary

In this chapter, we have looked at the basics of the Spring Framework and different components of a Spring Web MVC. In the next chapter, we will bring things together and look at building our first RESTful application using Spring Boot.

CHAPTER 3

RESTful Spring

In this chapter, we will discuss the following:

- The basics of Spring Boot

- Building a Hello World REST application

- Tools for accessing REST applications

One of the Spring Framework's goals is to reduce plumbing code so that developers can focus their efforts on implementing core business logic. However, as the Spring Framework evolved and added several subprojects to its portfolio, developers ended up spending a considerable amount of time setting up projects, finding project dependencies, and writing boiler plate code and configuration.

Spring Boot, a Spring portfolio project, aims at simplifying Spring application bootstrapping by providing a set of starter project templates. These would pull all the proper dependencies that are needed based on project capabilities. For example, if you enable JPA capability, it automatically includes all the dependent JPA, Hibernate, and Spring JAR files.

Spring Boot also takes an opinionated approach and provides default configuration that simplifies application development quite a bit. For example, if Spring Boot finds JPA and MySQL JARs in the classpath, it would automatically configure a JPA Persistence Unit. It also enables creation of standalone Spring applications with embedded Jetty/ Tomcat servers, making them easy to deploy on any machine with just Java installed. Additionally, it provides production-ready features such as metrics and health checks. Throughout this book, we will be exploring and learning these and additional features of Spring Boot.

© Balaji Varanasi and Maxim Bartkov 2022
B. Varanasi and M. Bartkov, *Spring REST*, https://doi.org/10.1007/978-1-4842-7477-4_3

> **Note**   Spring Roo is another Spring portfolio project that attempts to provide rapid Spring application development. It provides a command line tool that enables easy project bootstrapping and generates code for components such as JPA entities, web controllers, test scripts, and necessary configuration. Although there was a lot of initial interest in the project, Spring Roo never really became mainstream. AspectJ code generation and a steep learning curve coupled with its attempt to take over your project are some reasons for lack of its adoption. Spring Boot, by contrast, takes a different approach; it focuses on jump-starting the project and providing clever, sensible, default configuration. Spring Boot doesn't generate any code that makes it easy to manage your project.

Generating a Spring Boot Project

It is possible to create a Spring Boot project from scratch. However, Spring Boot provides the following options to generate a new project:

- Use Spring Boot's starter website (`http://start.spring.io`).
- Use the Spring Tool Suite (STS) IDE.
- Use the Boot command line interface (CLI).

We will explore all three alternatives in this chapter. However, for the rest of the book, we will be opting for the Boot CLI to generate new projects. Before we start with project generation, it is important that Java is installed on your machine. Spring Boot requires that you have Java SDK 1.8 or higher installed. In this book we will be using Java 1.8.

Installing a Build Tool

Spring Boot supports the two most popular build systems: Maven and Gradle. In this book we will be using Maven as our build tool. Spring Boot requires Maven version 3.5 or higher. The steps to download and configure Maven on your Windows machine are given here. Similar instructions for Mac and other operating systems can be found on Maven's install page (`https://maven.apache.org/install.html`):

1. Download the latest Maven binary from `https://maven.apache.org/download.cgi`. At the time of writing this book, the current version of Maven was 3.8.1. For Windows, download the `apache-maven-3.8.1-bin.zip` file.

2. Unzip the contents of the zip file under `C:\tools\maven`.

3. Add an Environment variable `M2_HOME` with value `C:\tools\maven\apache-maven-3.8.1`. This tells Maven and other tools where Maven is installed. Also make sure that the `JAVA_HOME` variable is pointing to the installed JDK.

4. Append the value `%M2_HOME%\bin` to the `Path` environment variable. This allows you to run Maven commands from the command line.

5. Open a new command line and type the following:

```
mvn - v
```

You should see an output similar to Figure 3-1, indicating that Maven was successfully installed.

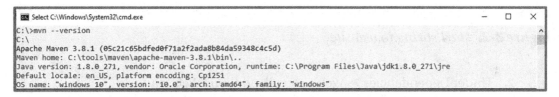

Figure 3-1. *Maven installation verification*

Note   To learn more about Maven, refer to *Introducing Maven*, published by Apress (`http://www.apress.com/9781484208427`).

Generating a Project Using start.spring.io

Spring Boot hosts an Initializr application at `http://start.spring.io`. The Initializr provides a web interface that allows you to enter project information and pick the capabilities needed for your project, and voilà—it generates the project as a zip file. Follow these steps to generate our Hello World REST application:

1. Launch the `http://start.spring.io` website in your browser and enter the information shown in Figure 3-2.

Figure 3-2. *start.spring.io website*

2. Under Dependencies ➤ Web, select the option "Web" and indicate that you would like Spring Boot to include web project infrastructure and dependencies.

3. Then hit the "Generate Project" button. This will begin the `hello-rest.zip` file download.

On completion of the download, extract the contents of the zip file. You will see the `hello-rest` folder generated. Figure 3-3 shows the contents of the generated folder.

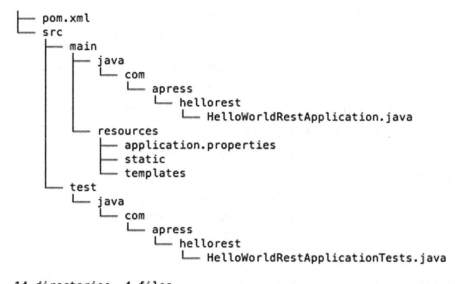

```
    ├── pom.xml
    └── src
        ├── main
        │   ├── java
        │   │   └── com
        │   │       └── apress
        │   │           └── hellorest
        │   │               └── HelloWorldRestApplication.java
        │   └── resources
        │       ├── application.properties
        │       ├── static
        │       └── templates
        └── test
            └── java
                └── com
                    └── apress
                        └── hellorest
                            └── HelloWorldRestApplicationTests.java

14 directories, 4 files
```

Figure 3-3. *hello-rest application contents*

A quick look at the hello-rest contents shows that we have a standard Maven-based Java project layout. We have the src\main\java folder, which houses Java source code; src\main\resources, which contains property files; static content, such as HTML\CSS\JS files; and the src\test\java folder, which contains the test cases. On running a Maven build, this project generates a JAR artifact. Now, this might be a little confusing for the first-timer who is used to WAR artifacts for deploying web applications. By default, Spring Boot creates standalone applications in which everything gets packaged into a JAR file. These applications will have embedded servlet containers such as Tomcat and are executed using a good old main() method.

Note   Spring Boot also allows you to work with WAR artifacts which contain html, css, js, and other files necessary for the development of web applications that can be deployed to external Web and application containers.

Listing 3-1 gives the contents of the hello-rest application's pom.xml file.

Listing 3-1. hello-rest pom.xml file Contents

```xml
<?xml version="1.0" encoding="UTF-8"?>
<project xmlns="http://maven.apache.org/POM/4.0.0" xmlns:xsi="http://www.
w3.org/2001/XMLSchema-instance"
    xsi:schemaLocation="http://maven.apache.org/POM/4.0.0 https://maven.
    apache.org/xsd/maven-4.0.0.xsd">
    <modelVersion>4.0.0</modelVersion>
    <parent>
        <groupId>org.springframework.boot</groupId>
        <artifactId>spring-boot-starter-parent</artifactId>
        <version>2.5.3</version>
        <relativePath/>
    </parent>
    <groupId>com.appress</groupId>
    <artifactId>hello-rest</artifactId>
    <version>0.0.1-SNAPSHOT</version>
    <name>Hello World REST</name>
    <description>Hello World REST Application Using Spring Boot
    </description>
    <properties>
        <java.version>1.8</java.version>
    </properties>
    <dependencies>
        <dependency>
            <groupId>org.springframework.boot</groupId>
            <artifactId>spring-boot-starter-web</artifactId>
        </dependency>
        <dependency>
            <groupId>org.springframework.boot</groupId>
            <artifactId>spring-boot-starter-test</artifactId>
            <scope>test</scope>
        </dependency>
    </dependencies>
```

```
<build>
      <plugins>
            <plugin>
                  <groupId>org.springframework.boot</groupId>
                  <artifactId>spring-boot-maven-plugin</artifactId>
            </plugin>
      </plugins>
</build>
</project>
      </build>
</project>
```

The groupId, artifactId, and version elements in the pom.xml file correspond to Maven's standard GAV coordinates describing our project. The parent tag indicates that we will be inheriting from the spring-boot-starter-parent POM. This ensures that our project inherits Spring Boot's default dependencies and versions. The dependencies element lists two POM file dependencies: spring-boot-starter-web and spring-boot-starter-test. Spring Boot uses the term **starter POMs** to describe such POM files.

These starter POMs are used to pull other dependencies and don't actually contain any code of their own. For example, the spring-boot-starter-web pulls Spring MVC dependencies, Tomcat-embedded container dependencies, and a Jackson dependency for JSON processing. These starter modules play an important role in providing needed dependencies and simplifying the application's POM file to just a few lines. Table 3-1 lists some of the commonly used starter modules.

Table 3-1. *Spring Boot Starter Modules*

Starter POM dependency	Use
spring-boot-starter	Starter that brings in core dependencies necessary for functions such as auto-configuration support and logging
spring-boot-starter-aop	Starter that brings in support for aspect-oriented programming and AspectJ
spring-boot-starter-test	Starter that brings in dependencies such as JUnit, Mockito, and spring-test necessary for testing

(continued)

Table 3-1. (*continued*)

Starter POM dependency	Use
`spring-boot-starter-web`	Starter that brings in MVC dependencies (`spring-webmvc`) and embedded servlet container support
`spring-boot-starter-data-jpa`	Starter that adds Java Persistence API support by bringing in `spring-data-jpa`, `spring-orm`, and Hibernate dependencies
`spring-boot-starter-data-rest`	Starter that brings in `spring-data-rest-webmvc` to expose repositories as REST API
`spring-boot-starter-hateoas`	Starter that brings in `spring-hateoas` dependencies for HATEOAS REST services
`spring-boot-starter-jdbc`	Starter for supporting JDBC databases

Finally, the `spring-boot-maven-plugin` contains goals for packaging the application as an executable JAR/WAR and running it.

The `HelloWorldRestApplication.java` class serves as the main class for our application and contains the `main()` method. Listing 3-2 shows the contents of the `HelloWorldRestApplication.java` class. The `@SpringBootApplication` annotation is a convenient annotation and is equivalent to declaring the following three annotations:

- `@Configuration`—Marks the annotated class as containing one or more Spring bean declarations. Spring processes these classes to create bean definitions and instances.

- `@ComponentScan`—This class tells Spring to scan and look for classes annotated with `@Component`, `@Service`, `@Repository`, `@Controller`, `@RestController`, and `@Configuration`. By default, Spring scans all the classes in the package where the `@ComponentScan` annotated class resides. To override the default behavior, we can set this annotation in the configuration class and define basePackages argument as the name of the package.

- @EnableAutoConfiguration—Enables Spring Boot's auto-configuration behavior. Based on the dependencies and configuration found in the classpath, Spring Boot intelligently guesses and creates bean configurations.

Typical Spring Boot applications always use these three annotations. In addition to providing a nice alternative in those scenarios, the @SpringBootApplication annotation correctly denotes the class's intent.

Listing 3-2. HelloWorldRestApplication Contents

```
package com.apress.hellorest;

import org.springframework.boot.SpringApplication;
import org.springframework.boot.autoconfigure.SpringBootApplication;

@SpringBootApplication
public class HelloWorldRestApplication {

    public static void main(String[] args) {
        SpringApplication.run(HelloWorldRestApplication.class, args);
    }
}
```

The main() method simply delegates the application bootstrapping to SpringApplication's run() method. run() takes a HelloWorldRestApplication. class as its argument and instructs Spring to read annotation metadata from HelloWorldRestApplication and populate ApplicationContext from it.

Now that we have looked at the generated project, let's create a REST endpoint that simply returns "Hello REST." Ideally, we would create this endpoint in a separate controller Java class. However, to keep things simple, we will create the endpoint in HelloWorldRestApplication, as shown in Listing 3-3. We start by adding the @RestController, indicating that HelloWorldRestApplication has possible REST endpoints. We then create the helloGreeting() method, which simply returns the greeting "Hello REST." Finally, we use the RequestMapping annotation to map web requests for "/greet" path to helloGreeting() handler method.

Listing 3-3. Hello REST Endpoint

```
package com.apress.hellorest;

import org.springframework.boot.SpringApplication;
import org.springframework.boot.autoconfigure.SpringBootApplication;
import org.springframework.web.bind.annotation.RestController;
import org.springframework.web.bind.annotation.RequestMapping;

@SpringBootApplication
@RestController
public class HelloWorldRestApplication {

    public static void main(String args) {
        SpringApplication.run(HelloWorldRestApplication.class, args);
    }

    @GetMapping("/greet")
    public String helloGreeting() {
        return "Hello REST";
    }

}
```

The next step is to launch and run our application. To do this, open a command line, navigate to the hello-rest folder, and run the following command:

```
mvn spring-boot:run
```

You will see Maven downloading the necessary plugins and dependencies, and then it will launch the application, as shown here:

```
  .   ____          _            __ _ _
 /\\ / ___'_ __ _ _(_)_ __  __ _ \ \ \ \
( ( )\___ | '_ | '_| | '_ \/ _` | \ \ \ \
 \\/  ___)| |_)| | | | | || (_| |  ) ) ) )
  '  |____| .__|_| |_|_| |_\__, | / / / /
 =========|_|==============|___/=/_/_/_/
[32m :: Spring Boot :: [39m                [2m (v2.5.3)[0;39m
```

[2m2021-08-12 21:54:43.147[0;39m [32m INFO[0;39m [35m15012[0;39m [2m---
[0;39m [2m[main][0;39m [36mc.a.hellorest.HelloWorldRestApplication
[0;39m [2m:[0;39m Starting HelloWorldRestApplication using Java 1.8 on
DESKTOP-82GK4GP with PID 15012 (C:\Users\makus\OneDrive\Desktop\hello-rest\
target\classes started by makus in C:\Users\makus\OneDrive\Desktop\hello-
rest)
[2m2021-08-12 21:54:43.149[0;39m [32m INFO[0;39m [35m15012[0;39m [2m---
[0;39m [2m[main][0;39m [36mc.a.hellorest.HelloWorldRestApplication
[0;39m [2m:[0;39m No active profile set, falling back to default profiles:
default
[2m2021-08-12 21:54:43.843[0;39m [32m INFO[0;39m [35m15012[0;39m [2m---
[0;39m [2m[main][0;39m [36mo.s.b.w.embedded.tomcat.TomcatWebServer
[0;39m [2m:[0;39m Tomcat initialized with port(s): 8080 (http)
[2m2021-08-12 21:54:43.851[0;39m [32m INFO[0;39m [35m15012[0;39m [2m---
[0;39m [2m[main][0;39m [36mo.apache.catalina.core.StandardService
[0;39m [2m:[0;39m Starting service [Tomcat]
[2m2021-08-12 21:54:43.851[0;39m [32m INFO[0;39m [35m15012[0;39m [2m--
-[0;39m [2m[main][0;39m [36morg.apache.catalina.core.
StandardEngine [0;39m [2m:[0;39m Starting Servlet engine: [Apache
Tomcat/9.0.50]
[2m2021-08-12 21:54:43.917[0;39m [32m INFO[0;39m [35m15012[0;39m [2m---
[0;39m [2m[main][0;39m [36mo.a.c.c.C.[Tomcat].[localhost].
[0;39m [2m:[0;39m Initializing Spring embedded WebApplicationContext
[2m2021-08-12 21:54:43.917[0;39m [32m INFO[0;39m [35m15012[0;39m [2m---
[0;39m [2m[main][0;39m [36mw.s.c.ServletWebServerApplicationCon
text[0;39m [2m:[0;39m Root WebApplicationContext: initialization completed
in 734 ms
[2m2021-08-12 21:54:44.286[0;39m [32m INFO[0;39m [35m15012[0;39m [2m---
[0;39m [2m[main][0;39m [36mo.s.b.w.embedded.tomcat.TomcatWebServer
[0;39m [2m:[0;39m Tomcat started on port(s): 8080 (http) with context
path ''
[2m2021-08-12 21:54:44.297[0;39m [32m INFO[0;39m [35m15012[0;39m [2m---
[0;39m [2m[main][0;39m [36mc.a.hellorest.HelloWorldRestApplication
[0;39m [2m:[0;39m Started HelloWorldRestApplication in 1.445 seconds (JVM
running for 2.055)

To test our running application, launch a browser and navigate to http://
localhost:8080/greet. Notice that Spring Boot launches the application as the Root
context and not the hello-world context. You should see a screen similar to that in
Figure 3-4.

Hello REST

Figure 3-4. Hello REST greeting

SPRING INITIALIZR

The Spring Initializr application hosted at http://start.spring.io itself is built using
Spring Boot. You can find the source code of this application on GitHub at https://github.
com/spring-io/initializr. It is also possible for you to build and host your own
instances of the Initializr application.

In addition to providing a web interface, the Initializr provides an HTTP endpoint that provides
similar project generation capability. In fact, Spring Boot's CLI and IDEs such as STS use this
HTTP endpoint behind the scenes for generating projects.

The HTTP endpoint can also be invoked from the command line using curl. For example,
the following command would generate the hello-rest project zip file using curl. The –d
options are used to provide data that gets passed as request parameters:

```
curl https://start.spring.io/starter.zip -d style=web -d name=hello-rest
```

Generating a Project Using STS

Spring Tool Suite or STS is a free Eclipse-based development environment that provides
great tooling support for developing Spring-based applications. You can download and
install the latest version of STS from Pivotal's website at https://spring.io/tools. At
the time of writing this book, the current version of STS was 4.11.0.

STS provides a user interface similar to Initializr's web interface for generating Boot starter projects. Here are the steps for generating a Spring Boot project:

1. Launch STS if you haven't already done so. Go to File ➤ New and click Spring Starter Project, as shown in Figure 3-5.

Figure 3-5. *STS Spring starter project*

2. In the following screen, enter the information as shown in Figure 3-6. Enter Maven's GAV information. Hit Next.

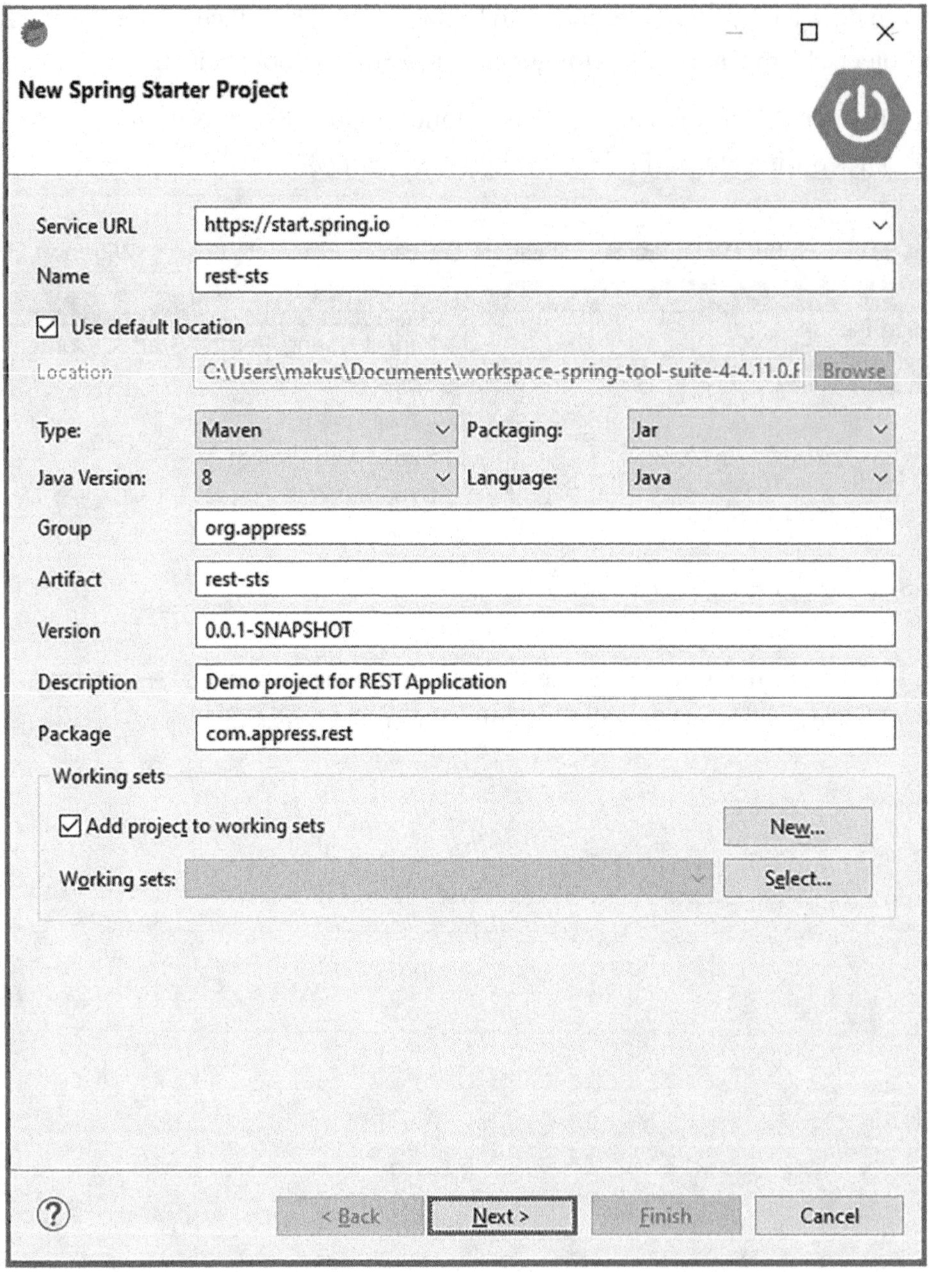

Figure 3-6. *Starter project options*

3. In the following screen, enter the information as shown in
    Figure 3-7. Select the web starter option. Hit Next.

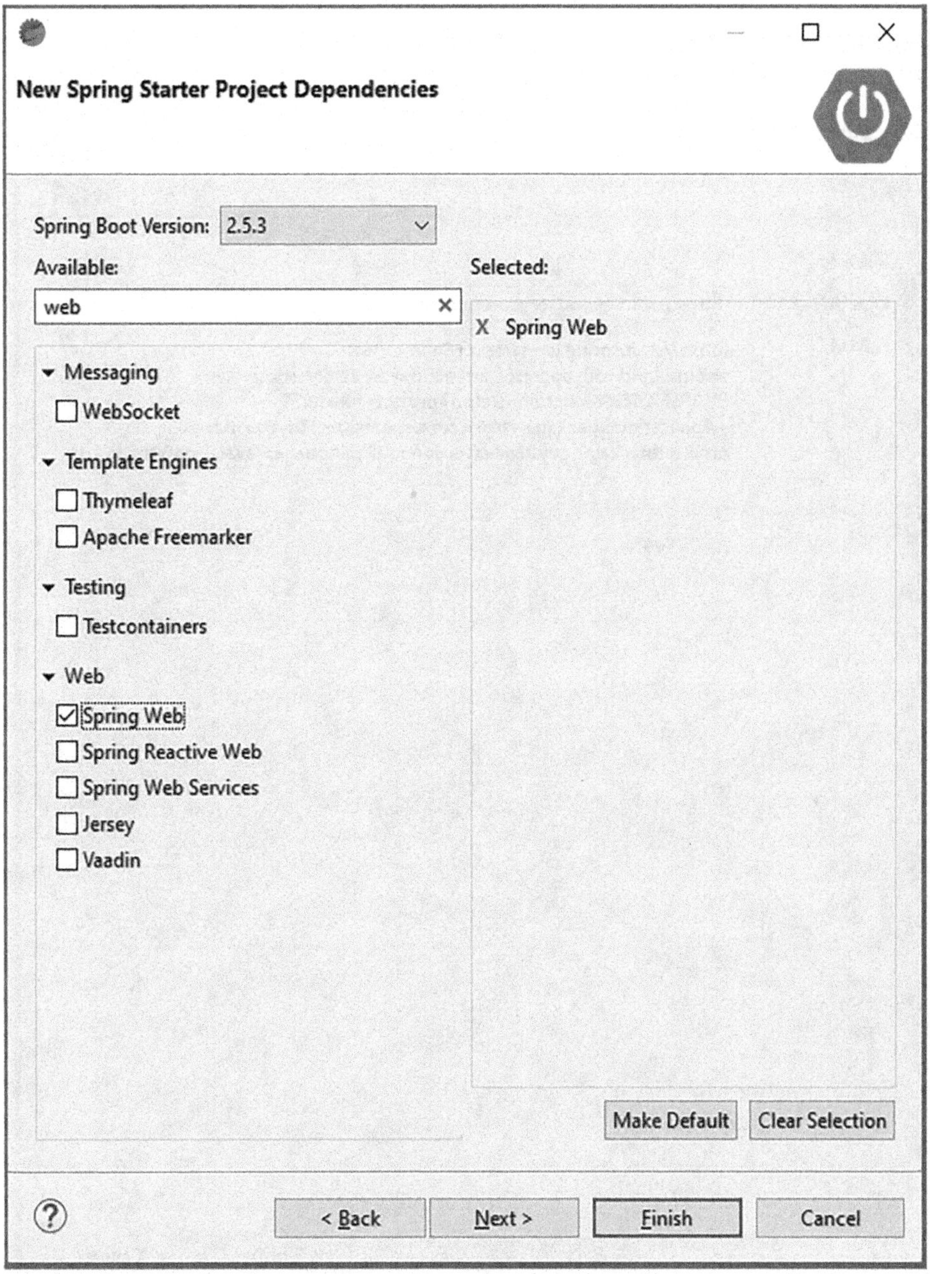

Figure 3-7. *Starter project options*

4. On the following screen, change the location where you would
    like to store the project. The "Full Url" area shows the HTTP REST
    endpoint along with the options that you selected (see Figure 3-8).

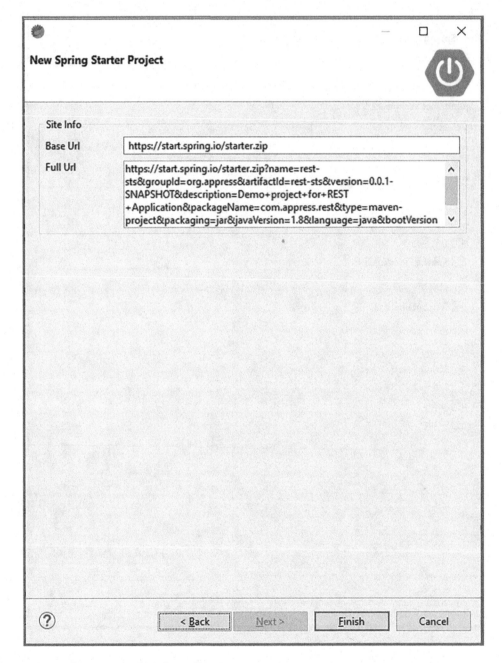

Figure 3-8. *Starter project location*

5. Hit the Finish button and you will see the new project created in STS. The contents of the project are similar to the project that we created earlier (see Figure 3-9).

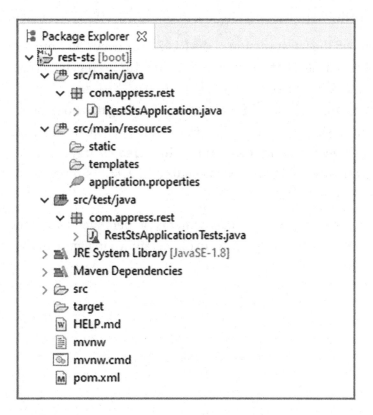

Figure 3-9. *STS Spring starter project resources*

STS's starter project wizard provides a convenient way to generate new Spring Boot projects. The newly created project automatically gets imported into the IDE and is immediately available for development.

Generating a Project Using the CLI

Spring Boot provides a command line interface (CLI) for generating projects, prototyping, and running Groovy scripts. Before we can start using the CLI, we need to install it. Here are the steps for installing the Boot CLI on a Windows machine:

1. Download the latest version of the CLI ZIP distribution from Spring's website at `https://docs.spring.io/spring-boot/docs/current/reference/html/getting-started.html#getting-started.installing.cli`. At the time of writing this book, the current version of CLI was 2.5.3. This version can be downloaded directly from `https://repo.spring.io/release/org/springframework/boot/spring-boot-cli/2.5.3/spring-boot-cli-2.5.3-bin.zip`.

2. Extract the zip file and place its contents (folders such as `bin` and `lib`) under `C:\tools\springbootcli`, as shown in Figure 3-10.

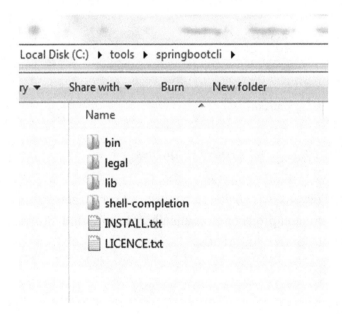

Figure 3-10. *Spring Boot CLI contents*

3. Add a new environment variable `SPRING_HOME` with value `c:\tools\springbootcli`.

4. Edit the `Path` environment variable, and add the `%SPRING_HOME%/bin` value to its end.

5. Open a new command line and verify the installation running the following command:

```
spring --version
```

You should see an output similar to that shown in Figure 3-10.

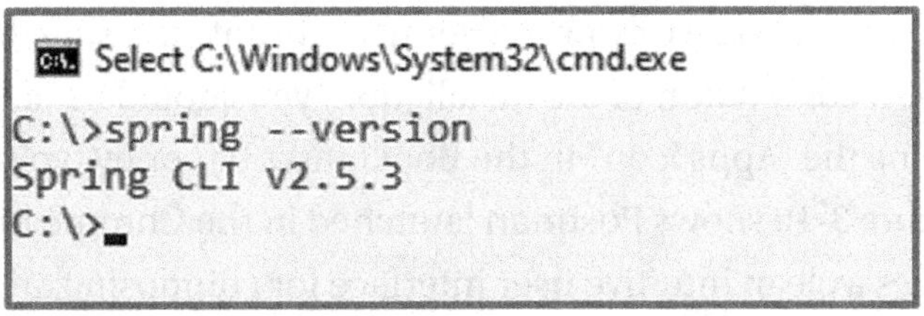

Figure 3-11. *Spring Boot CLI installation*

Now that we have the Boot CLI installed, generating a new project simply involves running the following command at the command line:

```
spring init --dependencies web rest-cli
```

The command creates a new `rest-cli` project with web capability. The output of running the command is shown in Listing 3-4.

Listing 3-4. Boot CLI Output

```
C:\test>spring init --dependencies web rest-cli
Using service at https://start.spring.io
Project extracted to 'C:\test\rest-cli'
```

Accessing REST Applications

There are several free and commercial tools that allow you to access and experiment with REST API/applications. In this section we will look at some of the popular tools that allow you to quickly test a request and inspect the response.

Postman

Postman is a Chrome browser extension for making HTTP requests. It offers a plethora of features that makes it easy to develop, test, and document a REST API. A Chrome app version of Postman is also available that provides additional features such as bulk uploading that are not available in the browser extension.

Postman can be downloaded and installed from the Chrome Web Store. To install Postman, simply launch the Chrome browser and navigate to `https://chrome.google.com/webstore/detail/postman/fhbjgbiflinjbdggehcddcbncdddomop`. You might be asked to log in to your Google Chrome account and confirm using the "New app" installation dialog. On completion of the installation, you should be able to locate and launch Postman using the "Apps icon" in the Bookmarks bar or by typing `chrome://apps/shortcut`. Figure 3-10 shows Postman launched in the Chrome browser.

Postman provides a clean intuitive user interface for composing an HTTP request, sending it to a server, and viewing the HTTP response. It also automatically saves the requests, which are readily available for future runs. Figure 3-12 shows an HTTP GET request made to our Greet service and its response. You can also see the request saved in the History section of the left sidebar.

Figure 3-12. *Postman browser extension*

Postman makes it easy to logically group related API calls into **collections**, as shown in Figure 3-12. It is possible to have subcollections of requests under a collection.

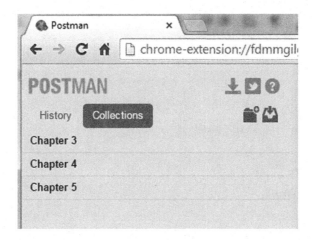

Figure 3-13. *Postman collections*

RESTClient

RESTClient is a Firefox extension for accessing REST APIs and applications. Unlike Postman, RESTClient doesn't have a lot of bells and whistles, but it provides basic functionality to quickly test a REST API. To install RESTClient, launch the Firefox browser and navigate to the URL `https://addons.mozilla.org/en-US/firefox/addon/restclient/`. Then click the "+ Add to Firefox" button, and in the following "Software Installation" dialog, click the "Install Now" button.

On completion of the installation, you can launch RESTClient using the RESTClient icon ▣ on the top right corner of the browser. Figure 3-14 shows the RESTClient application with a request to our Greet service and the corresponding response.

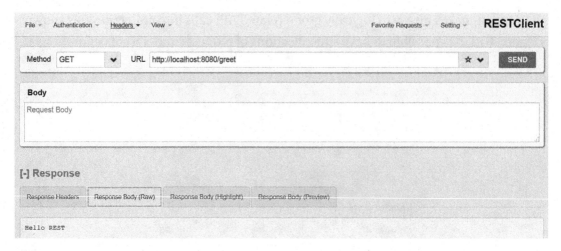

Figure 3-14. *RESTClient*

Summary

Spring Boot provides an opinionated approach to building Spring-based applications. In this chapter, we looked at Spring Boot's features and used it to build a Hello World REST application. We also looked at the Postman and RESTClient tools for testing and exploring the REST API.

In the next chapter, we will begin working on a more complex REST application and discuss the process of identifying and designing resources.

CHAPTER 4

Beginning QuickPoll Application

In this chapter we will discuss the following:

- Analyzing the requirements for QuickPoll

- Identifying QuickPoll resources

- Designing representations

- Implementing QuickPoll

Up to this point, we have looked at the fundamentals of REST and reviewed our technology choice of implementation—Spring MVC. Now it's time to develop a more complex application. In this chapter, we will introduce you to the beginnings of an application that we will be working on throughout this book. We will call it QuickPoll. We will go through the process of analyzing the requirements, identifying resources, designing their representation, and, finally, providing an implementation to a subset of features. In the upcoming chapters, we will continue our design and implementation by adding new features, documentation, security, and versioning.

Introducing QuickPoll

Polls have become a popular option for soliciting views and opinions from the community on many websites these days. There are a couple of variations between online polls, but a poll typically has a question and a list of answers, as shown in Figure 4-1.

© Balaji Varanasi and Maxim Bartkov 2022
B. Varanasi and M. Bartkov, *Spring REST*, https://doi.org/10.1007/978-1-4842-7477-4_4

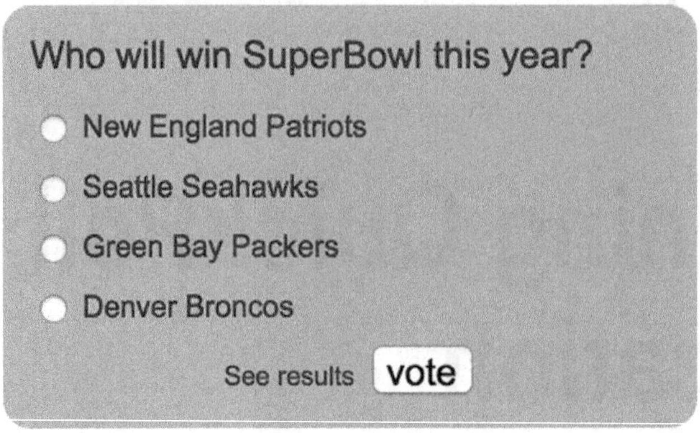

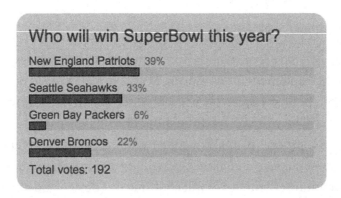

Figure 4-1. *Web poll example*

Participants vote and communicate their opinion by selecting one or more responses. Many polls also allow participants to view the poll results, as shown in Figure 4-2.

Figure 4-2. *Web poll results*

Imagine being part of QuickPoll Inc., a budding Software as a Service (or SaaS) provider that allows users to create, manipulate, and vote on polls. We plan to launch our services to a small audience, but we intend to become a global enterprise. In addition to the Web, QuickPoll would also like to target native iOS and Android platforms. To achieve these lofty goals, we have chosen to implement our application using REST principles and web technologies.

We begin the development process by analyzing and understanding requirements. Our QuickPoll application has the following requirements:

- Users interact with QuickPoll services to create new polls.

- Each poll contains a set of options that are provided during poll creation.

- Options inside a poll can be updated at a later point.

- To keep things simple, QuickPoll restricts voting on a single option.

- Participants can cast any number of votes.

- Results of a poll can be viewed by anyone.

We have started with a simple set of requirements for QuickPoll. As with any other application, these requirements will evolve and change. We will address those changes in the upcoming chapters.

Designing QuickPoll

As discussed in Chapter 1, designing a RESTful application typically involves the following steps:

1. Resource identification

2. Resource representation

3. Endpoint identification

4. Verb/action identification

Resource Identification

We begin the resource identification process by analyzing requirements and extracting *nouns*. At a high level, the QuickPoll application has *users* that create and interact with *polls*. From the previous statement, you can identify User and Poll as nouns and classify them as resources. Similarly, users can vote on polls and view the voting results, making Vote another resource. This resource modeling process is similar to database modeling in that it is used to identify entities or object-oriented design that identifies domain objects.

It is important to remember that all nouns identified need not be exposed as resources. For example, a poll contains several options, making Option another candidate for resource. Making Poll Option a resource would require a client to make two GET requests. The first request will obtain a Poll representation; the second request will obtain an associated Options representation. However, this approach makes the API chatty and might overload servers. An alternative approach is to include the options inside a Poll representation, thereby hiding Option as a resource. This would make Poll a coarse-grained resource, but clients would get poll-related data in one call. Additionally, the second approach can enforce business rules such as requiring at least two options for a poll to be created.

This *noun* approach allows us to identify collection resources. Now, consider the scenario in which you want to retrieve all of the votes for a given poll. To handle this, you need a "votes" collection resource. You can perform a GET request and obtain the entire collection. Similarly, we need a "polls" collection resource, which allows us to query groups of polls and create new ones.

Finally, we need to address the scenario in which we count all of the votes for a poll and return the computed results to the client. This involves looping through all the votes for a poll, grouping those votes based on options, and then counting them. Such processing operations are typically implemented using a "controller" resource, which we introduced in Chapter 1. In this case, we model a *ComputeResult* resource, which performs this counting operation. Table 4-1 shows the identified resources and their collection resource counterparts.

Table 4-1. *Resources for QuickPoll Application*

Resource	Description
User	Singleton User Resource
Users	Collection User Resource
Poll	Singleton Poll Resource
Polls	Collection Poll Resource
Vote	Singleton Vote Resource
Votes	Collection Vote Resource
ComputeResult	Count Processing Resource

Resource Representation

The next step in the REST API design process is defining resource representations and representation formats. REST APIs typically support multiple formats such as HTML, JSON, and XML. The choice of the format largely depends on the API audience. For example, a REST service that is internal to the company might only support JSON format, whereas a public REST API might speak XML and JSON formats. In this chapter and in the rest of the book, JSON will be the preferred format for our operations.

JSON FORMAT

The JavaScript Object Notation, or JSON, is a lightweight format for exchanging information. Information in JSON is organized around two structures: objects and arrays.

A JSON object is a collection of name/value pairs. Each name/value pair consists of a field name in double quotes followed by a colon (:), followed by a field value. JSON supports several types of values such as Boolean (true or false), number (int or float), String, null, arrays, and object. Examples of name/value pairs include

```
"country" : "US"
"age" : 31
 "isRequired" : true
"email" : null
```

JSON objects are surrounded by curly braces ({}), and each name/value pair is separated using a comma (,). Here is an example of a person JSON object:

```
{ "firstName": "John", "lastName": "Doe", "age" : 26, "active" : true }
```

The other JSON structure, an array, is an ordered collection of values. Each array is surrounded by square brackets ([ ]), with values separated by a comma. Here is an example of an array of locations:

```
[ "Salt Lake City", "New York", "Las Vegas", "Dallas"]
```

JSON arrays can also contain objects as their values:

71

```
[
            { "firstName": "Jojn", "lastName": "Doe", "age": 26, "active": true },
            { "firstName": "Jane", "lastName": "Doe", "age": 22, "active": true },
            { "firstName": "Jonnie", "lastName": "Doe", "age": 30, "active": false }
]
```

Resources are made up of set of attributes that can be identified using a process similar to object-oriented design. A Poll resource, for example, has a question attribute, containing a Poll question, and an id attribute, which uniquely identifies the Poll. It also contains a set of options; each option is made up of a value and an id. Listing 4-1 shows a representation of a Poll with sample data.

Listing 4-1. Poll Representation

```
{

        "id": 2,
        "question": "How will win SuperBowl this year?",

"options": [{"id": 45, "value": "New England Patriots"}, {"id": 49,
"value": "Seattle Seahawks"}, {"id": 51, "value": "Green Bay Packers"},
{"id": 54, "value": "Denver Broncos"}]
}
```

Note   We are intentionally excluding a user from Poll representation in this chapter. In Chapter 8, we will discuss user representation along with its associations to Poll and Vote resources.

The representation of a Poll collection resource contains a collection of individual polls. Listing 4-2 gives the representation of a Polls collection resource with dummy data.

Listing 4-2. List of Polls Representation

```
[

        {
        "id": 5,
        "question": "q1",
```

```
        "options": [
{"id": 6, "value": "X"}, {"id": 9, "value": "Y"},
{"id": 10, "value": "Z"}]
        },
        {
        "id": 2,
        "question": "q10",
        "options": [{"id": 15, "value": "Yes"}, {"id": 16, "value": "No"}]
        }
        . . . . . . .
]
```

The Vote resource contains the option for which the vote was cast and a unique identifier. Listing 4-3 shows the Vote resource representation with dummy data.

Listing 4-3. Vote Representation

```
{
        "id": 245,
        "option": {"id": 45, "value": "New England Patriots"}
}
```

Listing 4-4 gives the Votes collection resource representation with dummy data.

Listing 4-4. List of Votes Representation

```
[
        {
        "id": 245,
        "option": {"id": 5, "value": "X"}
    },
    {
        "id": 110,
         "option": {"id": 7, "value": "Y"}
    },
        . . . . . . . . . . . .
```

The ComputeResult resource representation should include the total number of votes and Poll options along with the vote count associated with each option. Listing 4-5 shows this representation with sample data. We use the totalVotes attribute to hold the cast votes and the results attribute to hold the option id and the associated votes.

Listing 4-5. ComputeResult Representation

```
{
    totalVotes: 100,
    "results" : [
                { "id" : 1, "count" : 10 },
                { "id" : 2, "count" : 8 },
                { "id" : 3, "count" : 6 },
                { "id" : 4, "count" : 4 }
            ]
}
```

Now that we have defined our resource representation, we will move on to identifying endpoints for those resources.

Endpoint Identification

REST resources are identified using URI endpoints. Well-designed REST APIs should have endpoints that are understandable, intuitive, and easy to use. Remember that we build REST APIs for our consumers to use. Hence, the names and the hierarchy that we choose for our endpoints should be unambiguous to consumers.

We design the endpoints for our service using best practices and conventions widely used in the industry. The first convention is to use a base URI for our REST service. The base URI provides an entry point for accessing the REST API. Public REST API providers typically use a subdomain such as http://api.domain.com or http://dev.domain.com as their base URI. Popular examples include GitHub's https://api.github.com and Twitter's https://api.twitter.com. By creating a separate subdomain, you prevent any possible name collisions with webpages. It also allows you to enforce security policies that are different from the regular website. To keep things simple, we will be using http://localhost:8080 as our base URI in this book.

The second convention is to name resource endpoints using plural nouns. In our QuickPoll application, this would result in an endpoint `http://localhost:8080/polls` for accessing the Poll collection resource. Individual Poll resources will be accessed using a URI such as `http://localhost:8080/polls/1234` and `http://localhost:8080/polls/3456`. We can generalize access to individual Poll resources using the URI template `http://localhost:8080/polls/{pollId}`. Similarly, the endpoints `http://localhost:8080/users` and `http://localhost:8080/users/{userId}` are used for accessing collection and individual User resources.

The third convention advises using a URI hierarchy to represent resources that are related to each other. In our QuickPoll application, each Vote resource is related to a Poll resource. Because we typically cast votes for a Poll, a hierarchical endpoint `http://localhost:8080/polls/{pollId}/votes` is recommended for obtaining or manipulating all the votes associated with a given Poll. In the same way, the endpoint `http://localhost:8080/polls/{pollId}/votes/{voteId}` would return an individual vote that was cast for the Poll.

Finally, the endpoint `http://localhost:8080/computeresult` can be used to access the ComputeResult resource. For this resource to function properly and count the votes, a poll id is required. Because the `ComputeResult` works with `Vote`, `Poll`, and `Option` resources, we can't use the third approach for designing a URI that is hierarchal in nature. For use cases like these that require data to perform computation, the fourth convention recommends using a query parameter. For example, a client can invoke the endpoint `http://localhost:8080/computeresult?pollId=1234` to count all of the votes for the Poll with id 1234. Query parameters are an excellent vehicle for providing additional information to a resource.

In this section, we have identified the endpoints for the resources in our QuickPoll application. The next step is to identify the actions that are allowed on these resources, along with the expected responses.

Action Identification

HTTP verbs allow clients to interact and access resources using their endpoints. In our QuickPoll application, the clients must be able to perform one or more CRUD operations on resources such as Poll and Vote. Analyzing the use cases from the "Introducing QuickPoll" section, Table 4-2 shows the operations allowed on Poll/Polls collection resources along with the success and error responses. Notice that on the Poll collection resource, we allow GET and POST operations but deny PUT and Delete operations. A POST on the collection resource allows the client to create new polls. Similarly, we allow GET, PUT, and Delete operations on a given Poll resource but deny POST operation. The service returns a 404 status code for any GET, PUT, and DELETE operation on a Poll resource that doesn't exist. Similarly, any server errors would result in a status code of 500 sent to the client.

Table 4-2. *Allowed Operations on a Poll Resource*

HTTP method	Resource endpoint	Input	Success response	Error response	Description
GET	/polls	Body: empty	Status: 200 Body: poll list	Status: 500	Retrieves all available polls
POST	/polls	Body: new poll data	Status: 201 Body: newly created poll id	Status: 500	Creates a new poll
PUT	/polls	N/A	N/A	Status: 400	Forbidden action
Delete	/polls	N/A	N/A	Status: 400	Forbidden action
GET	/polls/ {pollId}	Body: empty	Status: 200 Body: poll data	Status: 404 or 500	Retrieves an existing poll
POST	/polls/ {pollId}	N/A	N/A	Status: 400	Forbidden
PUT	/polls/ {pollId}	Body: poll data with updates	Status: 200 Body: empty	Status: 404 or 500	Updates an existing poll
Delete	/polls/ {pollId}	Body: empty	Status: 200	Status: 404 or 500	Deletes an existing poll

In the same fashion, Table 4-3 shows the operations allowed on Vote/Votes collection resources.

Table 4-3. *Allowed Operations on Vote Resource*

HTTP method	Resource endpoint	Input	Success response	Error response	Description
GET	/polls/ {pollId}/ votes	Body: empty	Status: 200 Body: votes list	Status: 500	Retrieves all available votes for a given poll
POST	/polls/ {pollId}/ votes	Body: new vote	Status: 201 Body: newly created vote id	Status: 500	Creates a new vote
PUT	/polls/ {pollId}/ votes	N/A	N/A	Status: 400	Forbidden action
Delete	/polls/ {pollId}/ votes	N/A	N/A	Status: 400	Forbidden action
GET	/polls/ {pollId}/ votes/ {voteId}	Body: empty	Status: 200 Body: vote data	Status: 404 or 500	Retrieves an existing vote
POST	/polls/ {pollId}/ votes/ {voteId}	N/A	N/A	Status: 400	Forbidden
PUT	/polls/ {pollId}/ votes/ {voteId}	N/A	N/A	Status: 400	Forbidden as a casted vote can't be updated according to our requirements
Delete	/polls/ {pollId}/ votes/ {voteId}	N/A	N/A	Status: 400	Forbidden as a casted vote can't be deleted according to our requirements

Finally, Table 4-4 shows the operations allowed on the ComputeResult resource.

Table 4-4. *Allowed Operations on ComputeResult Resource*

HTTP method	Resource endpoint	Input	Success response	Error response	Description
GET	/computeresult	Body: empty Param: pollId	Status: 200 Body: vote count	Status: 500	Returns the vote count for the given poll

This concludes the design for the QuickPoll REST service. Before we start our implementation, we will review QuickPoll's high-level architecture.

QuickPoll Architecture

The QuickPoll application will be made of a web or REST API layer and a repository layer with a domain layer (layer between Web API and repository) crosscutting those two, as depicted in Figure 4-3. A layered approach provides a clear separation of concerns, making applications easy to build and maintain. Each layer interacts with the following layer using a well-defined contract. As long as the contract is maintained, it is possible to swap out underlying implementations without any impact on the overall system.

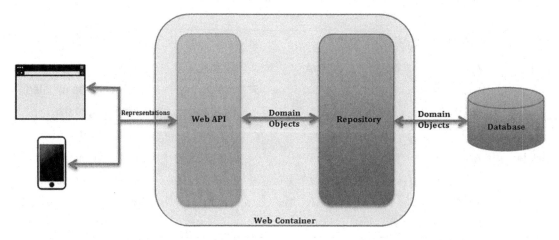

Figure 4-3. *QuickPoll architecture*

The Web API layer is responsible for receiving client requests, validating user input, interacting with a service or a repository layer, and generating a response. Using HTTP protocol, resource representations are exchanged between clients and the Web API layer. This layer contains controllers/handlers and is typically very lightweight as it delegates most of the work to layers beneath it.

The domain layer is considered to be the "heart" of an application. Domain objects in this layer contain business rules and business data. These objects are modeled after the nouns in the system. For example, a Poll object in our QuickPoll application would be considered a domain object.

The repository or data access layer is responsible for interacting with a datastore such as a database or LDAP or a legacy system. It typically provides CRUD operations for storing and retrieving objects from/to a datastore.

Note   Observant readers will notice that the QuickPoll architecture is missing a service layer. Service layer typically sits between the API/presentation layer and repository layer. It contains coarse-grained API with methods that fulfill one or more use cases. It is also responsible for managing transactions and other crosscutting concerns such as security.

Because we are not dealing with any complex use cases for QuickPoll application in this book, we will not be introducing service layers into our architecture.

Implementing QuickPoll

We begin QuickPoll implementation by generating a Spring Boot project using STS. Follow the steps discussed in the "Generating a Project Using STS" section of Chapter 3, and create a project named quick-poll. Figures 4-4 and 4-5 give the configuration information used during project generation. Notice that we have selected the "JPA" and "Web" options.

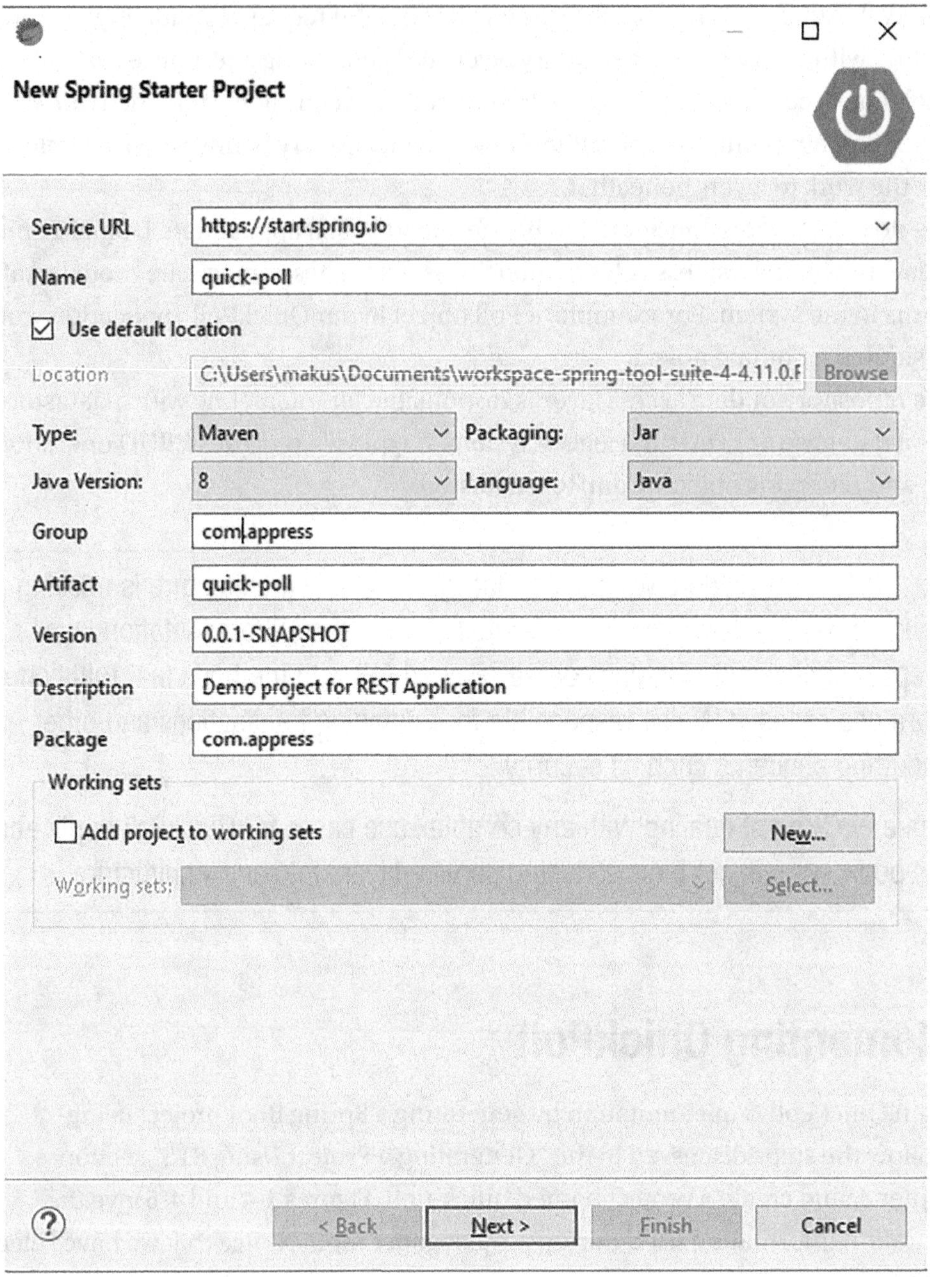

Figure 4-4. *QuickPoll spring starter project*

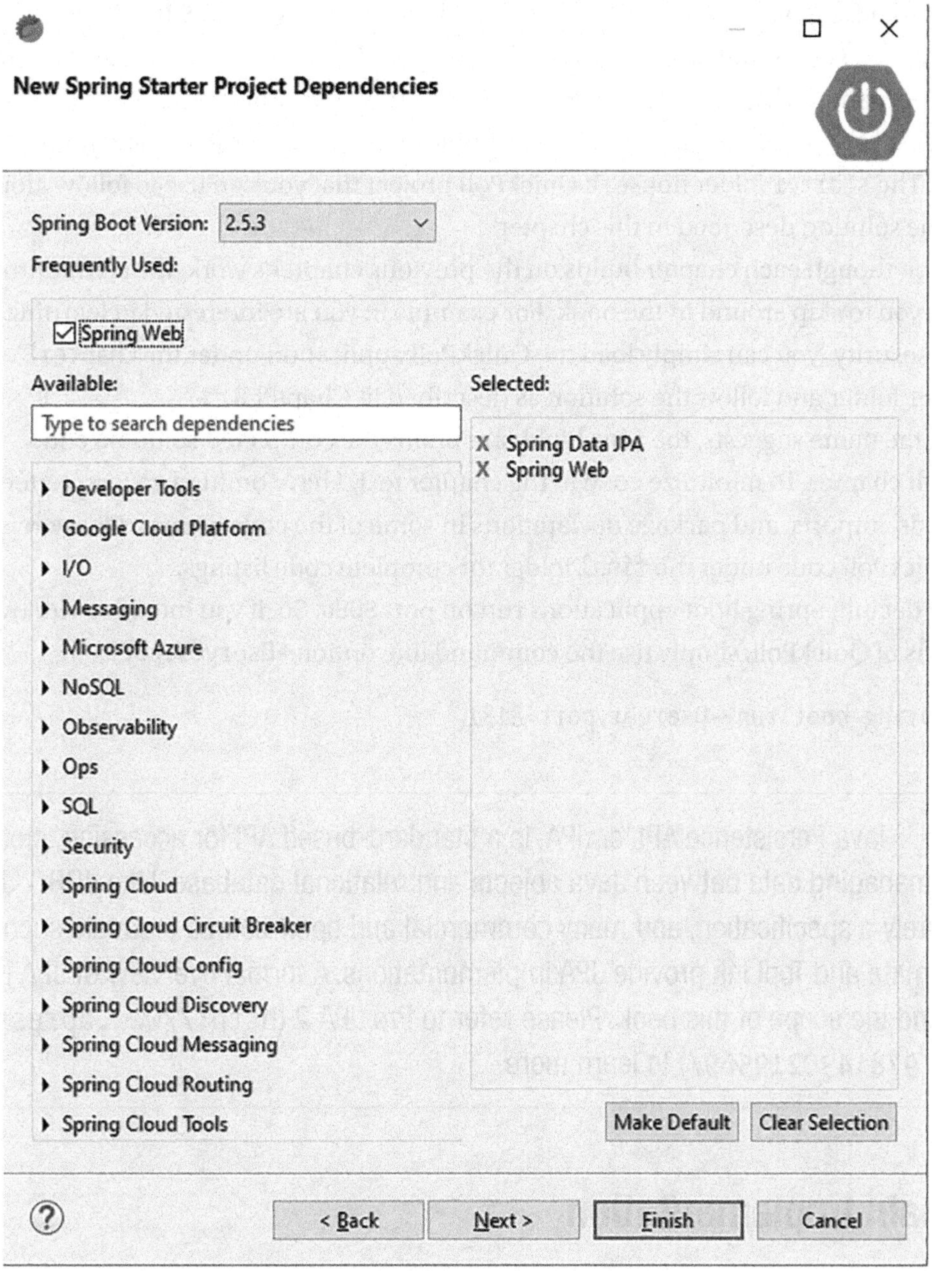

Figure 4-5.   QuickPoll Spring starter project dependencies

Alternatively, you can import the QuickPoll project into your STS IDE from the downloaded source code for this book. The downloaded source code contains a number of folders named ChapterX, in which X represents the corresponding chapter number. Each ChapterX folder further contains two subfolders: a starter folder and a final folder. The starter folder houses a QuickPoll project that you can use to follow along with the solution described in this chapter.

Even though each chapter builds on the previous chapter's work, the starter project allows you to skip around in the book. For example, if you are interested in learning about security, you can simply load the QuickPoll application under the Chapter8\ starter folder and follow the solution as described in Chapter 8.

As the name suggests, the final folder contains the completed solution/code for each chapter. To minimize code in the chapter text, I have omitted getters/setters methods, imports, and package declarations in some of the code listings. Please refer to the QuickPoll code under the final folder for complete code listings.

By default, Spring Boot applications run on port 8080. So, if you intend to run two versions of QuickPoll, simply use the command line option -Dserver.port:

```
mvn spring-boot:run -Dserver.port=8181
```

Note   Java Persistence API, or JPA, is a standard-based API for accessing, storing, and managing data between Java objects and relational database. Like JDBC, JPA is purely a specification, and many commercial and open-source products such as Hibernate and TopLink provide JPA implementations. A formal overview of JPA is beyond the scope of this book. Please refer to Pro JPA 2 (http://www.apress.com/9781430219569/) to learn more.

Domain Implementation

The domain objects typically act as a backbone for any application. So, the next step in our implementation process is to create domain objects. Figure 4-5 shows a UML Class diagram representing the three domain objects in our QuickPoll application and their relationships.

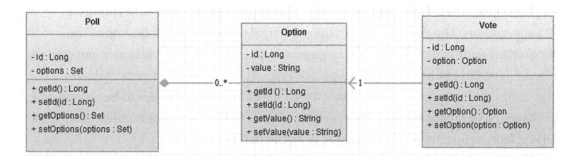

Figure 4-6. *QuickPoll domain objects*

Inside the quick-poll project, create a `com.apress.domain` subpackage under the `/src/main/java` folder, and create Java classes corresponding to the domain objects that we identified. Listing 4-6 gives the implementation of the `Option` class. As you can see, the `Option` class has two fields: `id`, to hold the identity; and `value`, corresponding to the option value. Additionally, you will see that we have annotated this class with JPA annotations such as `@Entity` and `@Id`. This allows instances of the `Option` class to be easily persisted and retrieved using JPA technology.

Listing 4-6. Option Class

```
package com.apress.domain;

import javax.persistence.Column;
import javax.persistence.Entity;
import javax.persistence.GeneratedValue;
import javax.persistence.Id;

@Entity
public class Option {

    @Id
    @GeneratedValue
    @Column(name="OPTION_ID")
    private Long id;

    @Column(name="OPTION_VALUE")
    private String value;

    // Getters and Setters omitted for brevity
}
```

Next, we create a `Poll` class, as shown in Listing 4-7, along with corresponding JPA annotations. The `Poll` class has a question field to store the poll question. The `@OneToMany` annotation, as the name suggests, indicates that a `Poll` instance can contain zero or more `Option` instances. The `CascadeType.All` indicates that any database operations such as persist, remove, or merge on a `Poll` instance needs to be propagated to all related `Option` instances. For example, when a `Poll` instance gets deleted, all of the related `Option` instances will be deleted from the database.

Listing 4-7. Poll Class

```java
package com.apress.domain;

import java.util.Set;
import javax.persistence.CascadeType;
import javax.persistence.Column;
import javax.persistence.Entity;
import javax.persistence.GeneratedValue;
import javax.persistence.Id;
import javax.persistence.JoinColumn;
import javax.persistence.OneToMany;
import javax.persistence.OrderBy ;

@Entity
public class Poll {

        @Id
        @GeneratedValue
        @Column(name="POLL_ID")
        private Long id;

        @Column(name="QUESTION")
        private String question;

        @OneToMany(cascade=CascadeType.ALL)
        @JoinColumn(name="POLL_ID")
        @OrderBy
        private Set<Option> options;

        // Getters and Setters omitted for brevity
}
```

Finally, we create the Vote class, as shown in Listing 4-8. The @ManyToOne annotation indicates that an Option instance can have zero or more Vote instances associated with it.

Listing 4-8. Vote Class

```
package com.apress.domain;

import javax.persistence.Column;
import javax.persistence.Entity;
import javax.persistence.GeneratedValue;
import javax.persistence.Id;
import javax.persistence.JoinColumn;
import javax.persistence.ManyToOne;

@Entity
public class Vote {

        @Id
        @GeneratedValue
        @Column(name="VOTE_ID")
        private Long id;

        @ManyToOne
        @JoinColumn(name="OPTION_ID")
        private Option option;

        // Getters and Setters omitted for brevity
}
```

Repository Implementation

Repositories, or data access objects (DAO), provide an abstraction for interacting with datastores. Repositories traditionally include an interface that provides a set of finder methods such as findById, findAll for retrieving data, and methods to persist and delete data. Repositories also include a class that implements this interface using datastore-specific technologies. For example, a repository dealing with a database uses technology such as JDBC or JPA, and a repository dealing with LDAP would use JNDI. It is also customary to have one repository per domain object.

Although this has been a popular approach, there is a lot of boilerplate code that gets duplicated in each repository implementation. Developers attempt to abstract common functionality into a generic interface and generic implementation (http://www.ibm.com/developerworks/library/j-genericdao/). However, they are still required to create a pair of repository interfaces and classes for each domain object. Often these interfaces and classes are empty and just result in more maintenance.

The Spring Data project aims at addressing this problem by completely eliminating the need to write any repository implementations. With Spring Data, all you need is a repository interface to automatically generate its implementation at runtime. The only requirement is that application repository interfaces should extend one of the many available Spring Data marker interfaces. Because we will be persisting our QuickPoll domain objects into a relational database using JPA, we will be using Spring Data JPA subproject's org.springframework.data.repository.CrudRepository marker interface. As you can see from Listing 4-9, the CrudRepository interface takes the type of domain object that it manipulates and the type of domain object's identifier field as its generic parameters T and ID.

Listing 4-9. CrudRepository API

```
public interface CrudRepository<T, ID> extends Repository<T, ID> {
        <S extends T> S save(S var1);

        <S extends T> Iterable<S> saveAll(Iterable<S> var1);

        Optional<T> findById(ID var1);

        Iterable<T> findAll();

        Iterable<T> findAllById(Iterable<ID> var1);

        void deleteById(ID var1);

        void delete(T var1);

        void deleteAllById(Iterable<? extends ID> var1);

        void deleteAll(Iterable<? extends T> var1);

        void deleteAll();
```

```
    // Utility Methods
    long count();
    boolean existsById(ID var1);
}
```

We begin our repository implementation by creating a `com.apress.repository` package under the `src\main\java` folder. Then, we create an `OptionRepository` interface as shown in Listing 4-10. As discussed earlier, the `OptionRepository` extends Spring Data's `CrudRepository` and thereby inherits all of its CRUD methods. Because the `OptionRepository` works with the `Option` domain object, it passes `Option` and `Long` as generic parameter values.

Listing 4-10. OptionRepository Interface

```
package com.apress.repository;

import org.springframework.data.repository.CrudRepository;
import com.apress.domain.Option;

public interface OptionRepository extends CrudRepository<Option, Long> {

}
```

Taking the same approach, we then create `PollRepository` and `VoteRepository` interfaces, as shown in Listings 4-11 and 4-12.

Listing 4-11. PollRepository Interface

```
public interface PollRepository extends CrudRepository<Poll, Long> {

}
```

Listing 4-12. OptionRepository Interface

```
public interface VoteRepository extends CrudRepository<Vote, Long> {

}
```

Embedded Database

In the previous section, we created repositories, but we need a relational database for persisting data. The relational database market is full of options ranging from commercial databases such as Oracle and SQL Server to open-source databases such as MySQL and PostgreSQL. To speed up our QuickPoll application development, we will be using HSQLDB, a popular in-memory database. In-memory, aka embedded, databases don't require any additional installations and can simply run as a JVM process. Their quick startup and shutdown capabilities make them ideal candidates for prototyping and integration testing. At the same time, they don't usually provide a persistent storage and the application needs to seed the database every time it bootstraps.

Spring Boot provides excellent support for HSQLDB-, H2-, and Derby-embedded databases. The only requirement is to include a build dependency in the pom.xml file. Spring Boot takes care of starting the database during deployment and stopping it during application shutdown. There is no need to provide any database connection URLs or username and password. Listing 4-13 shows the dependency information that needs to be added to QuickPoll's pom.xml file.

Listing 4-13. HSQLDB POM.XML Dependency

```
<dependency>
    <groupId>org.hsqldb</groupId>
    <artifactId>hsqldb</artifactId>
    <scope>runtime</scope>
</dependency>
```

API Implementation

In this section, we will create Spring MVC controllers and implement our REST API endpoints. We begin by creating the com.apress.controller package under src\main\ java to house all of the controllers.

PollController Implementation

The PollController provides all of the necessary endpoints to access and manipulate the Poll and Polls resources. Listing 4-14 shows a bare-bones PollController class.

Listing 4-14. PollController Class

```
package com.apress.controller;

import javax.inject.Inject;
import org.springframework.web.bind.annotation.RestController;
import com.apress.repository.PollRepository;

@RestController
public class PollController {

        @Inject
        private PollRepository pollRepository;

}
```

The `PollController` class is annotated with a `@RestController` annotation. The `@RestController` is a convenient yet meaningful annotation and has the same effect as adding both `@Controller` and `@ResponseBody` annotations. Because we need to read and store `Poll` instances, we use the `@Inject` annotation to inject an instance of `PollRepository` into our controller. The `javax.inject.Inject` annotation introduced as part of Java EE 6 provides a standard mechanism for declaring dependencies. We use this annotation in favor of Spring's proprietary `@Autowired` annotation to be more compliant. In order to use the `@Inject` annotation, we need to add the dependency shown in Listing 4-15 to the `pom.xml` file.

Listing 4-15. Inject Dependency in POM File

```
<dependency>
        <groupId>javax.inject</groupId>
        <artifactId>javax.inject</artifactId>
        <version>1</version>
</dependency>
```

A GET request on the `/polls` endpoint provides a collection of all of the polls available in the QuickPolls application. Listing 4-16 shows the necessary code for implementing this functionality. The `shortcut` annotation declares the URI and the allowed HTTP method. The `getAllPolls` method used `ResponseEntity` as its return type, indicating that the return value is the complete HTTP response. `ResponseEntity` gives you full control over the HTTP response, including the response body and response headers. The method implementation begins with reading all of the polls using the PollRepository. We then create an instance of ResponseEntity and pass in Poll data and the HttpStatus.OK status value. The Poll data becomes part of the response body and OK (code 200) becomes the response status code.

Listing 4-16. GET Verb Implementation for /polls

```
@GetMapping("/polls")
public ResponseEntity<Iterable<Poll>> getAllPolls() {
        Iterable<Poll> allPolls = pollRepository.findAll();
        return new ResponseEntity<>(pollRepository.findAll(), HttpStatus.OK);
}
```

Let's quickly test our implementation by running the QuickPoll application. In a command line, navigate to the quick-poll project directory and run the following command:

```
mvn spring-boot:run
```

Launch the Postman app in your Chrome browser and enter the URL http://localhost:8080/polls, as shown in Figure 4-7, and hit Send. Because we don't have any polls created yet, this command would result in an empty collection.

Normal	Basic Auth	Digest Auth	OAuth 1.0	No environment ▾		

GET All Polls

http://localhost:8080/polls		GET ▾	☑ URL params	☑ Headers (0)
Header	Value		Manage presets	
Send Save Preview Add to collection				Reset

Figure 4-7. *Get All Polls request*

Note   The downloaded source code contains an exported Postman collection with requests that can be used to run tests in this chapter. Simply import this collection into your Postman application and start using it.

The next stop for us is to implement capability to add new polls to the PollController. We accomplish this by implementing the POST verb functionality, as shown in Listing 4-17. The createPoll method takes a parameter of the type Poll. The @RequestBody annotation tells Spring that the entire request body needs to be converted to an instance of Poll. Spring uses the incoming Content-Type header to identify a proper message converter and delegates the actual conversion to it. Spring Boot comes with message converters that support JSON and XML resource representations. Inside the method, we simply delegate the Poll persistence to PollRepository's save method. We then create a new ResponseEntity with status CREATED (201) and return it.

Listing 4-17. Implementation to Create New Poll

```
@PostMapping("/polls")
public ResponseEntity<?> createPoll(@RequestBody Poll poll) {

        poll = pollRepository.save(poll);
        return new ResponseEntity<>(null, HttpStatus.CREATED);
}
```

Although this implementation fulfills the request, the client has no way of knowing the URI of the newly created Poll. For example, if the client wants to share the newly created Poll to a social networking site, the current implementation will not suffice. A best practice is to convey the URI to the newly created resource using the Location HTTP header. Building the URI would require us to inspect the HttpServletRequest object to obtain information such as Root URI and context. Spring makes the URI generation process easy via its ServletUriComponentsBuilder utility class:

```
URI newPollUri = ServletUriComponentsBuilder
                    .fromCurrentRequest()
                    .path("/{id}")
                    .buildAndExpand(poll.getId())
                    .toUri();
```

The fromCurrentRequest method prepares the builder by copying information such as host, schema, port, and so on from the HttpServletRequest. The path method appends the passed-in path parameter to the existing path in the builder. In the case of the createPoll method, this would result in http://localhost:8080/polls/{id}. The buildAndExpand method would build a UriComponents instance and replace any path variables ({id} in our case) with passed-in value. Finally, we invoke the toUri method on the UriComponents class to generate the final URI. The complete implementation of the createPoll method is shown in Listing 4-18.

Listing 4-18. Complete Implementation of Create Poll

```
@PostMapping("/polls")
public ResponseEntity<?> createPoll(@RequestBody Poll poll) {

        poll = pollRepository.save(poll);

        // Set the location header for the newly created resource
        HttpHeaders responseHeaders = new HttpHeaders();
        URI newPollUri = ServletUriComponentsBuilder
                                .fromCurrentRequest()
                                .path("/{id}")
                                .buildAndExpand(poll.getId())
                                .toUri();
        responseHeaders.setLocation(newPollUri);

        return new ResponseEntity<>(null, responseHeaders, HttpStatus.
        CREATED);
}
```

To test our newly added functionality, start the QuickPoll application. If you have the application already running, you need to terminate the process and restart it. Enter the information in Postman as shown in Figure 4-8 and hit Send. Make sure that you have added the Content-Type header with value application/json. The JSON used in the body is shown here:

```
{
    "question": "Who will win SuperBowl this year?",
    "options": [
                {"value": "New England Patriots"},
                {"value": "Seattle Seahawks"},
                {"value": "Green Bay Packers"},
                {"value": "Denver Broncos"}]
}
```

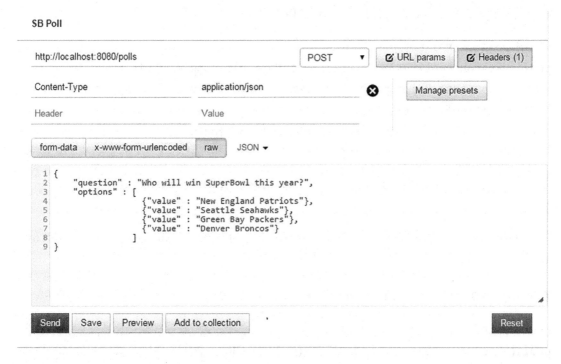

Figure 4-8. *Create Poll Postman example*

On completion of the request, you will see a Status 201 Created message and headers:

```
Content-Length ® 0
Date ® Mon, 23 Feb 2015 00:05:11 GMT
Location ® http://localhost:8080/polls/1
Server ® Apache-Coyote/1.1
```

Now let's turn our attention to accessing an individual poll. Listing 4-19 gives the necessary code. The value attribute in shortcut annotations (@GetMapping, @PostMapping, etc.) takes a URI template /polls/{pollId}. The placeholder {pollId} along with the @PathVarible annotation allows Spring to examine the request URI path and extract the pollId parameter value. Inside the method, we use the PollRepository's findById finder method to read the poll and pass it as part of a ResponseEntity.

Listing 4-19. Retrieving an Individual Poll

```
@GetMapping("/polls/{pollId}")
public ResponseEntity<?> getPoll(@PathVariable Long pollId) {
        Optional<Poll> poll = pollRepository.findById(pollId);
        if(!poll.isPresent()) {
                throw new Exception("Pool not found");

        }
        return new ResponseEntity<>(poll.get(), HttpStatus.OK);
}
```

In the same fashion, we implement the functionality to update and delete a Poll, as shown in Listing 4-20.

Listing 4-20. Update and Delete a Poll

```
@PutMapping("/polls/{pollId}")
public ResponseEntity<?> updatePoll(@RequestBody Poll poll, @PathVariable
Long pollId) {
        // Save the entity
        Poll newPoll = pollRepository.save(poll);
        return new ResponseEntity<>(HttpStatus.OK);
}

@DeleteMapping("/polls/{pollId}")
public ResponseEntity<?> deletePoll(@PathVariable Long pollId) {
        pollRepository.deleteById(pollId);
        return new ResponseEntity<>(HttpStatus.OK);
}
```

Once you have this code added to the `PollController`, restart the QuickPoll application and execute the Postman request as shown in Figure 4-8 to create a new poll. Then input the information in Figure 4-9 to create a new Postman request and update the poll. Notice that the PUT request contains the entire `Poll` representation along with IDs.

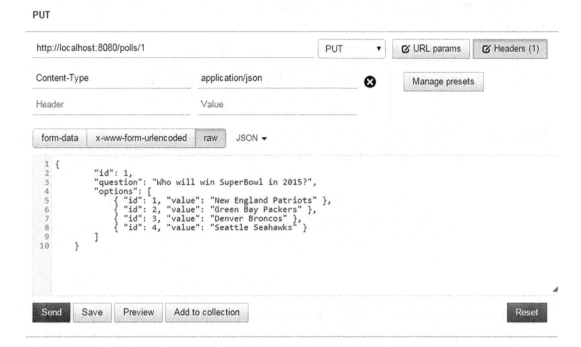

Figure 4-9. *Update poll*

This concludes the implementation of the `PostController`.

VoteController Implementation

Following the principles used to create PollController, we implement the
VoteController class. Listing 4-21 gives the code for the VoteController class along
with the functionality to create a vote. The VoteController uses an injected instance of
VoteRepository to perform CRUD operations on Vote instances.

Listing 4-21. VoteController Implementation

```
@RestController
public class VoteController {
        @Inject
        private VoteRepository voteRepository;

        @PostMapping("/polls/{pollId}/votes")
```

```
public ResponseEntity<?> createVote(@PathVariable Long pollId, @RequestBody
Vote vote) {
                vote = voteRepository.save(vote);

                // Set the headers for the newly created resource
                HttpHeaders responseHeaders = new HttpHeaders();

responseHeaders.setLocation(ServletUriComponentsBuilder.
fromCurrentRequest().path("/{id}").buildAndExpand(vote.getId()).toUri());

                return new ResponseEntity<>(null, responseHeaders,
                HttpStatus.CREATED);
        }
}
```

To test the voting capabilities, POST a new Vote to the /polls/1/votes endpoint with an option in the request body, as shown in Figure 4-10. On successful request execution, you will see a Location response header with value http://localhost:8080/ polls/1/votes/1.

Create Vote

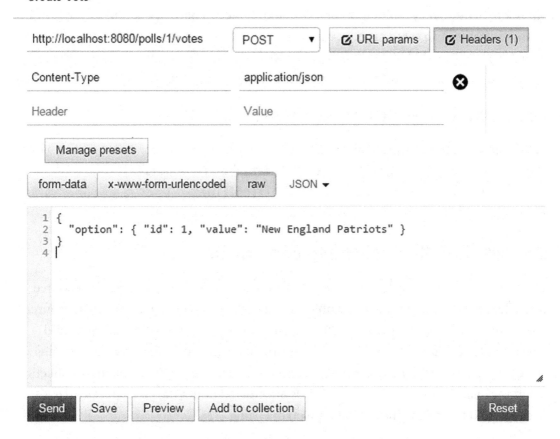

Figure 4-10. *Cast a new vote*

Next, we look at implementing the capability to retrieve all votes for a given poll. The findAll method in the VoteRepository returns all votes in the database. Because this would not meet our needs, we need to add this functionality to the VoteRepository as shown in Listing 4-22.

Listing 4-22. Modified VoteRepository Implementation

```
import org.springframework.data.jpa.repository.Query;

public interface VoteRepository extends CrudRepository<Vote, Long> {

@Query(value="select v.* from Option o, Vote v where o.POLL_ID = ?1 and
v.OPTION_ID = o.OPTION_ID", nativeQuery = true)
        public Iterable<Vote> findByPoll(Long pollId);
}
```

The custom finder method `findVotesByPoll` takes the ID of the `Poll` as its parameter. The `@Query` annotation on this method takes a native SQL query along with the `nativeQuery` flag set to `true`. At runtime, Spring Data JPA replaces the `?1` placeholder with the passed-in `pollId` parameter value. Next, we implement the `/polls/{pollId}/votes` endpoint in the `VoteController`, as shown in Listing 4-23.

Listing 4-23. GET All Votes Implementation

```
@GetMapping("/polls/{pollId}/votes")
public Iterable<Vote> getAllVotes(@PathVariable Long pollId) {
        return voteRepository. findByPoll(pollId);
}
```

ComputeResultController Implementation

The final piece remaining for us is the implementation of the `ComputeResult` resource. Because we don't have any domain objects that can directly help generate this resource representation, we implement two data transfer objects or DTOs—`OptionCount` and `VoteResult`. The `OptionCount` DTO contains the ID of the option and a count of votes casted for that option. The `VoteResult` DTO contains the total votes cast and a collection of `OptionCount` instances. These two DTOs are created under the `com.apress.dto` package, and their implementation is given in Listing 4-24.

Listing 4-24. DTOs for ComputeResult Resources

```
package com.apress.dto;
public class OptionCount {
        private Long optionId;
        private int count;
        // Getters and Setters omitted for brevity
}

package com.apress.dto;
import java.util.Collection;
```

```
public class VoteResult {
        private int totalVotes;
        private Collection<OptionCount> results;
        // Getters and Setters omitted for brevity
}
```

Following the principles used in creating the PollController and VoteController, we create a new ComputeResultController class, as shown in Listing 4-25. We inject an instance of VoteRepository into the controller, which is used to retrieve votes for a given poll. The computeResult method takes pollId as its parameter. The @RequestParam annotation instructs Spring to retrieve the pollId value from an HTTP query parameter. The computed results are sent to the client using a newly created instance of ResponseEntity.

Listing 4-25. ComputeResultController implementation

```
package com.apress.controller;

@RestController
public class ComputeResultController {

        @Inject
        private VoteRepository voteRepository;

        @GetMapping("/computeresult")
        public ResponseEntity<?> computeResult(@RequestParam Long pollId) {
                VoteResult voteResult = new VoteResult();
                Iterable<Vote> allVotes = voteRepository.
                findByPoll(pollId);
                // Algorithm to count votes

                return new ResponseEntity<VoteResult>(voteResult,
                HttpStatus.OK);
        }
}
```

There are several ways to count votes associated with each option. This code provides one such option:

```
int totalVotes = 0;
Map<Long, OptionCount> tempMap = new HashMap<Long, OptionCount>();
for(Vote v : allVotes) {
        totalVotes ++;
        // Get the OptionCount corresponding to this Option
        OptionCount optionCount = tempMap.get(v.getOption().getId());
        if(optionCount == null) {
                optionCount = new OptionCount();
                optionCount.setOptionId(v.getOption().getId());
                tempMap.put(v.getOption().getId(), optionCount);
        }
        optionCount.setCount(optionCount.getCount()+1);
}
voteResult.setTotalVotes(totalVotes);
voteResult.setResults(tempMap.values());
```

This concludes the ComputeResult controller implementation. Start/restart the QuickPoll application. Using the earlier Postman requests, create a poll and cast votes on its options. Then create a new Postman request as shown in Figure 4-11 and submit it to test our /computeresult endpoint.

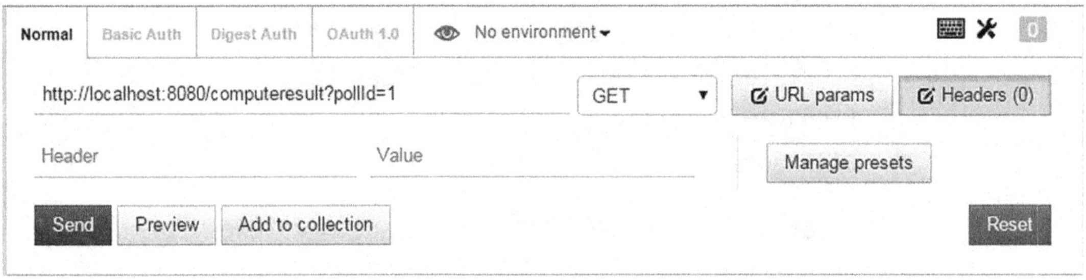

Figure 4-11.   *ComputeResult endpoint test*

On successful completion, you will see an output similar to this:

```
{
    "totalVotes": 7,
    "results": [
        {
            "optionId": 1,
            "count": 4
        },
        {
            "optionId": 2,
            "count": 3
        }
    ]
}
```

Summary

In this chapter, we looked at creating RESTful services for the QuickPoll application. Most of our examples in this chapter assumed a "happy path" in which everything goes as planned. However, this rarely happens in the real world. In the next chapter, we will look at handling errors, validating input data, and communicating meaningful error messages.

CHAPTER 5

Error Handling

In this chapter we will discuss the following:

- Handling errors in a REST API

- Designing meaningful error responses

- Validating API inputs

- Externalizing error messages

Error handling is one of the most important yet somewhat overlooked topics for programmers. Although we develop software with good intent, things do go wrong, and we must be prepared to handle and communicate those errors gracefully. The communication aspect is especially important to developers consuming a REST API. Well-designed error responses allow consuming developers to understand the issues and help them to use the API correctly. Additionally, good error handling allows API developers to log information that can aid in debugging issues on their end.

QuickPoll Error Handling

In our QuickPoll application, consider the scenario in which a user tries to retrieve a poll that doesn't exist. Figure 5-1 shows the Postman request for a nonexistent poll with id 100.

Non Existent Poll

http://localhost:8080/polls/100		GET ▼
Header	Value	Manage presets

| Send | Save | Preview | Add to collection |

Figure 5-1. *Requesting a nonexistent poll*

© Balaji Varanasi and Maxim Bartkov 2022
B. Varanasi and M. Bartkov, *Spring REST*, https://doi.org/10.1007/978-1-4842-7477-4_5

On receiving the request, the PollController in our QuickPoll application uses PollRepository to retrieve the poll. Because a poll with id 100 doesn't exist, PollRepository's findById method returns an empty Option and the PollController sends an empty body to the client, as shown in Figure 5-2.

Figure 5-2. *Response to a nonexistent poll*

Note   In this chapter, we will continue working on the QuickPoll application that we built in the previous chapter. The code is also available under the Chapter5\ starter folder of the downloaded source code. The completed solution is available under the Chapter5\final folder. As we have omitted getter/setter methods and imports in some of the listings in this chapter, please refer to the code under the final folder for complete listings. The Chapter5 folder also contains an exported Postman collection containing REST API requests associated with this chapter.

This current implementation is deceptive, as the client receives a status code 200. Instead, a status code 404 should be returned, indicating that the requested resource doesn't exist. To achieve this correct behavior, we will validate the poll id in the com. apress.controller.PollController's getPoll method and, for nonexistent polls, throw a com.apress.exception.ResourceNotFoundException exception. Listing 5-1 shows the modified getPoll implementation.

Listing 5-1. getPoll Implementation

```
@GetMapping("/polls/{pollId}")
public ResponseEntity<?> getPoll(@PathVariable Long pollId) {
        Optional<Poll> poll = pollRepository.findById(pollId);
```

```
    if(!poll.isPresent()) {
            throw new ResourceNotFoundException("Poll with id " +
            pollId + " not found");
    }
    return new ResponseEntity<>(poll.get(), HttpStatus.OK);
}
```

The ResourceNotFoundException is a custom exception, and its implementation is shown in Listing 5-2. Notice that an @ResponseStatus annotation is declared at the class level. The annotation instructs Spring MVC that an HttpStatus NOT_FOUND (404 code) should be used in the response when a ResourceNotFoundException is thrown.

Listing 5-2. ResourceNotFoundException Implementation

```
package com.apress.exception;

import org.springframework.http.HttpStatus;
import org.springframework.web.bind.annotation.ResponseStatus;

@ResponseStatus(HttpStatus.NOT_FOUND)
public class ResourceNotFoundException extends RuntimeException {

        private static final long serialVersionUID = 1L;

        public ResourceNotFoundException() {}

        public ResourceNotFoundException(String message) {
                super(message);
        }

        public ResourceNotFoundException(String message, Throwable cause) {
                super(message, cause);
        }
}
```

With these modifications in place, start the QuickPoll application, and run the Postman request for poll with ID 100. The PollController returns the right status code as shown in Figure 5-3.

Non Existent Poll

Figure 5-3. *New response for a nonexistent poll*

In addition to GET, other HTTP methods such as PUT, DELETE, and PATCH act on existing Poll resources. Hence, we need to perform the same poll ID validation in the corresponding methods so that we return the right status code to the client. Listing 5-3 shows the poll id verification logic encapsulated into a PollController's verifyPoll method along with the modified getPoll, updatePoll, and deletePoll methods.

Listing 5-3. Updated PollController

```java
protected Poll verifyPoll(Long pollId) throws ResourceNotFoundException {
        Optional<Poll> poll = pollRepository.findById(pollId);
        if(!poll.isPresent()) {
                throw new ResourceNotFoundException("Poll with id " +
                pollId + " not found");
        }
        return poll.get();
}

@GetMapping("/polls/{pollId}")
public ResponseEntity<?> getPoll(@PathVariable Long pollId) {
        return new ResponseEntity<>(verifyPoll(pollId), HttpStatus.OK);
}
```

```
@PutMapping("/polls/{pollId}")
public ResponseEntity<?> updatePoll(@RequestBody Poll poll, @PathVariable
Long pollId) {
        verifyPoll(pollId);
        pollRepository.save(poll);
        return new ResponseEntity<>(HttpStatus.OK);
}

@DeleteMapping("/polls/{pollId}")
public ResponseEntity<?> deletePoll(@PathVariable Long pollId) {
        pollRepository.deleteById(pollId);
        pollRepository.delete(pollId);
        return new ResponseEntity<>(HttpStatus.OK);
}
```

Error Responses

HTTP status codes play an important role in REST APIs. API developers should strive to return the right codes indicating the request status. Additionally, it is good practice to provide helpful, fine-grained details regarding the error in the response body. These details will enable API consumers to troubleshoot issues easily and help them to recover. As you can see in Figure 5-3, Spring Boot follows this practice and includes the following details in error response bodies:

- Timestamp—The time in milliseconds when the error happened.

- Status—HTTP status code associated with the error; this is partly redundant as it is same as the response status code.

- Error—The description associated with the status code.

- Exception—The fully qualified path to the exception class resulting in this error.

- Message—The message providing more details about the error.

- Path—The URI that resulted in the exception.

These details are generated by the Spring Boot framework. This feature is not available out of the box in non-Boot Spring MVC applications. In this section, we will implement a similar error response for a QuickPoll application using generic Spring MVC components so that it works in both Boot and non-Boot environments. Before we dive into this implementation, let's look at the error response details of two popular applications: GitHub and Twilio. Figure 5-4 shows GitHub's error response details for a request containing invalid inputs. The message attribute gives a plain description of the error, and the error attribute lists the fields with invalid inputs. In this example, the client's request is missing the Issue resource's title field.

```
HTTP/1.1 422 Unprocessable Entity
Content-Length: 149

{
  "message": "Validation Failed",
  "errors": [
    {
      "resource": "Issue",
      "field": "title",
      "code": "missing_field"
    }
  ]
}
```

Figure 5-4. *GitHub error response*

Twilio provides an API that allows developers programmatically make phone calls, send texts, and receive texts. Figure 5-5 shows the error response for a POST call that is missing a "To" phone number. The status and message fields are similar to fields in Spring Boot's response. The code field contains a numeric code that can be used to find more information about the exception. The more_info field contains the URL for error code documentation. On receiving this error, a Twilio API consumer can navigate to https://www.twilio.com/docs/errors/21201 and get more information to troubleshoot the error.

```
1  {
2        "status": 400,
3        "message": "No to number is specified",
4        "code": 21201,
5        "more_info": "http:\/\/www.twilio.com\/docs\/errors\/21201"
6  }
```

Figure 5-5. *Twilio error response*

It is clear that there is not a standard response format for errors. It is up to the API and framework implementers to decide on the details to be sent to the client. However, attempts to standardize the response format have begun, and an IETF specification known as Problem Details for HTTP APIs (`http://tools.ietf.org/html/draft-nottingham-http-problem-06`) is gaining traction. Inspired by the "Problem Details for HTTP APIs" specification, Listing 5-4 shows the error response format that we will be implementing in our QuickPoll application.

Listing 5-4. QuickPoll Error Response Format

```
{
        "title" : "",
        "status" : "",
        "detail" : ",
        "timestamp" : "",
        "developerMessage: "",
        "errors": {}
}
```

Here is a brief description of the fields in the QuickPoll error response:

- Title—The `title` field provides a brief title for the error condition. For example, errors resulting as a result of input validation will have the title "Validation Failure." Similarly, an "Internal Server Error" will be used for internal server errors.

- Status—The `status` field contains the HTTP status code for the current request. Even though it is redundant to include status code in the response body, it allows API clients to look for all the information that it needs to troubleshoot in one place.

- Detail—The detail field contains a short description of the error. The information in this field is typically human readable and can be presented to an end user.

- Timestamp—The time in milliseconds when the error occurred.

- developerMessage—The developerMessage contains information such as exception class name or stack trace that is relevant to developers.

- Errors—The error field is used to report field validation errors.

Now that we have our error response defined, we are ready to modify QuickPoll application. We begin by creating a Java representation of the response details, as shown in Listing 5-5. As you can see, the ErrorDetail class is missing the errors field. We will be adding that functionality in the upcoming section.

Listing 5-5. Error Response Details Representation

```java
package com.apress.dto.error;

public class ErrorDetail {

        private String title;
        private int status;
        private String detail;
        private long timeStamp;
        private String developerMessage;

        // Getters and Setters omitted for brevity
}
```

Error handling is a crosscutting concern. We need an application-wide strategy that handles all of the errors in the same way and writes the associated details to the response body. As we discussed in Chapter 2, classes annotated with @ControllerAdvice can be used to implement such crosscutting concerns. Listing 5-6 shows the RestExceptionHandler class with an aptly named handleResourceNotFoundException method. Thanks to the @ExceptionHandler annotation, any time a ResourceNotFoundException is thrown by a controller, Spring MVC would invoke the RestExceptionHandler's handleResourceNotFoundException method. Inside this method, we create an instance of ErrorDetail and populate it with error information.

Listing 5-6. RestExceptionHandler Implementation

```
package com.apress.handler;

import java.util.Date;
import javax.servlet.http.HttpServletRequest;
import org.springframework.http.HttpStatus;
import org.springframework.http.ResponseEntity;
import org.springframework.web.bind.annotation.ControllerAdvice;
import org.springframework.web.bind.annotation.ExceptionHandler;
import com.apress.dto.error.ErrorDetail;
import com.apress.exception.ResourceNotFoundException;

@ControllerAdvice
public class RestExceptionHandler {

        @ExceptionHandler(ResourceNotFoundException.class)

public ResponseEntity<?> handleResourceNotFoundException(ResourceNotFoundEx
ception rnfe, HttpServletRequest request) {

                ErrorDetail errorDetail = new ErrorDetail();
                errorDetail.setTimeStamp(new Date().getTime());
                errorDetail.setStatus(HttpStatus.NOT_FOUND.value());
                errorDetail.setTitle("Resource Not Found");
                errorDetail.setDetail(rnfe.getMessage());
                errorDetail.setDeveloperMessage(rnfe.getClass().getName());

                return new ResponseEntity<>(errorDetail, null, HttpStatus.
                NOT_FOUND);
        }

}
```

To verify that our newly created handler works as expected, restart the QuickPoll application and submit a Postman request to a nonexistent poll with id 100. You should see an error response as shown in Figure 5-6.

Figure 5-6. *ResourceNotFoundException error response*

Input Field Validation

As a famous proverb goes, "garbage in, garbage out"; input field validation should be another area of emphasis in every application. Consider the scenario in which a client requests a new poll to be created but doesn't include the poll question in the request. Figure 5-7 shows a Postman request with a missing question and the corresponding response. Make sure that you set the Content-Type header to "application/json" before firing the Postman request. From the response, you can see that the poll still gets created. Creating a poll with a missing question can result in data inconsistencies and other bugs.

Figure 5-7. *Creating a poll with a missing question*

Spring MVC provides two options for validating user input. In the first option, we create a validator that implements the `org.springframework.validation.Validator` interface. Then we inject this validator into a controller and invoke validator's validate method manually to perform validation. The second option is to use the JSR 303 validation, an API intended to simplify field validation in any layer of the application. Considering the simplicity and the declarative nature of the framework, we will be using JSR 303 validation framework in this book.

You can read more about JSR 303 at `https://beanvalidation.org/1.0/spec`.

The JSR 303 and JSR 349 define specifications for the Bean Validation API (version 1.0 and 1.1, respectively). They provide a metadata model for JavaBean validation via a set of standardized validation constraints. Using this API, you annotate domain object properties with validation constraints such as `@NotNull` and `@Email`. Implementing frameworks enforce these constraints at runtime. In this book, we will be using

Hibernate Validator, a popular JSR 303/349 implementation framework. Table 5-1 shows some of the out-of-the-box validation constraints available with Bean Validation API. Additionally, it is possible to define your own custom constraints.

Table 5-1. *Bean Validation API Constraints*

Constraint	Description
NotNull	Annotated field must not have null value.
Null	Annotated field must be null.
Max	Annotated field value must be an integer value lower than or equal to the number specified in the annotation.
Min	Annotated field value must be an integer value greater than or equal to the number specified in the annotation.
Past	Annotated field must be a date in the past.
Future	Annotated field must be a date in the future.
Size	Annotated field must match the min and max boundaries specified in the annotation. For a field that is a Collection, the size of the Collection is matched against boundaries. For a String field, the length of the string is verified against boundaries.
Pattern	Annotated field must match the regular expression specified in the annotation.

To add validation capabilities to QuickPoll, we start by annotating the Poll class as shown in Listing 5-7. Because we want to make sure that each Poll has a question, we annotated the question field with an @NotEmpty annotation. The javax.validation. constraints.NotEmpty annotation is not part of JSR 303/349 API. Instead, it is part of Hibernate Validator; it ensures that the input string is not null and its length is greater than zero. Also, to make the experience of taking a poll simpler, we will restrict each poll to contain no fewer than two and no more than six options.

Listing 5-7. Poll Class Annotated with JSR 303 Annotations

```
@Entity
public class Poll {

        @Id
        @GeneratedValue
        @Column(name="POLL_ID")
        private Long id;

        @Column(name="QUESTION")
        @NotEmpty
        private String question;

        @OneToMany(cascade=CascadeType.ALL)
        @JoinColumn(name="POLL_ID")
        @OrderBy
        @Size(min=2, max = 6)
        private Set<Option> options;

        // Getters and Setters removed for brevity
}
```

We now move our attention to the com.apress.controller.PollController and add an @Valid annotation to the createPoll method's Poll parameter, as shown in Listing 5-8. The @Valid annotation instructs Spring to perform data validation after binding the user-submitted data. Spring delegates the actual validation to a registered Validator. With Spring Boot adding JSR 303/JSR 349 and Hibernate Validator jars to the classpath, the JSR 303/JSR 349 is enabled automatically and will be used to perform the validation.

Listing 5-8. PollController Annotated with @Valid Annotations

```
@GetMapping(value="/polls")
public ResponseEntity<?> createPoll(@Valid @RequestBody Poll poll) {
        poll = pollRepository.save(poll);

        // Set the location header for the newly created resource
        HttpHeaders responseHeaders = new HttpHeaders();
        URI newPollUri = ServletUriComponentsBuilder
```

```
                    .fromCurrentRequest()
                    .path("/{id}")
                    .buildAndExpand(poll.getId())
                    .toUri();
        responseHeaders.setLocation(newPollUri);

        return new ResponseEntity<>(null, responseHeaders, HttpStatus.
        CREATED);
}
```

On repeating the Postman request with a missing question as we did in Figure 5-7, you will see the operation fail with an error code 400, as shown in Figure 5-8. From the error response, notice that Spring MVC completed validating the input. On not finding the required question field, it threw a `MethodArgumentNotValidException` exception.

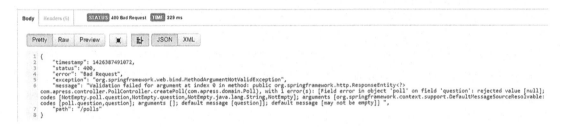

Figure 5-8. *Missing question resulting in error*

Even though Spring Boot's error message is helpful, to be consistent with our QuickPoll error response that we designed in Listing 5-4, we will modify the `RestExceptionHandler` so that we can intercept a `MethodArgumentNotValidException` exception and return an appropriate `ErrorDetail` instance. While we were designing the QuickPoll error response, we came up with an error field that can hold our validation errors. It is possible for a field to have one or more validation errors associated with it. For example, a missing question field in our Poll example would result in a "Field may not be null" validation error. In the same way, an empty email address could result in "Field may not be null" and "Field is not a well-formed email" validation errors. Keeping these validation constraints in mind, Listing 5-9 shows a complete error response with the validation error examples. The `error` object contains an unordered collection of key-value error instances. The error key represents the name of the resource feed that has validation errors. The error value is an array representing the validation error details.

From Listing 5-9, we can see that field1 contains one validation error and field2 is associated with two validation errors. Each validation error itself is made up of code that represents the violated constraint and a message containing a human-readable error representation.

Listing 5-9. Validation Error Format

```
{
        "title" : "",
        "status" : "",
        "detail" : ",
        "timestamp" : "",
        "path" : "",
        "developerMessage: "",
        "errors": {
                "field1" : [ {
                                "code" : "NotNull",
                                message" : "Field1 may not be null"
                        } ],
                "field2" : [ {
                                "code" : "NotNull",
                                "message" : "Field2 may not be null"
                        },
                        {
                                "code" : "Email",
                                "message" : "Field2 is not a well formed
                                email"
                        }]
                }
}
```

To represent the newly added validation error feature in the Java code, we created a new com.apress.dto.error.ValidationError class. Listing 5-10 shows the ValidationError class and updated ErrorDetail class. In order to generate the error response format shown in Listing 5-9, the error field in ErrorDetail class is defined as a Map that accepts String instances as keys and List of ValidationError instances as values.

Listing 5-10. ValidationError and Updated ErrorDetail Classes

```
package com.apress.dto.error;

public class ValidationError {

        private String code;
        private String message;

        // Getters and Setters removed for brevity
}

public class ErrorDetail {

        private String title;
        private int status;
        private String detail;
        private long timeStamp;
        private String path;
        private String developerMessage;

private Map<String, List<ValidationError>> errors = new HashMap<String,
List<ValidationError>>();

        // Getters and setters removed for brevity
}
```

The next step is to modify the RestExceptionHandler by adding a method that intercepts and processes the MethodArgumentNotValidException exception. Listing 5-11 shows the handleValidationError method implementation in RestExceptionHandler. We begin the method implementation by creating an instance of ErrorDetail and populating it. Then we use the passed-in exception parameter to obtain all the field errors and loop through the list. We created an instance of ValidationError for each field error and populated it with code and message information.

Listing 5-11. handleValidationError Implementation

```
@ControllerAdvice
public class RestExceptionHandler {

        @ExceptionHandler(MethodArgumentNotValidException.class)

public ResponseEntity<?> handleValidationError(MethodArgumentNotValidExcept
ion manve, HttpServletRequest request) {

                ErrorDetail errorDetail = new ErrorDetail();
                // Populate errorDetail instance
                errorDetail.setTimeStamp(new Date().getTime());
                errorDetail.setStatus(HttpStatus.BAD_REQUEST.value());

String requestPath = (String) request.getAttribute("javax.servlet.error.
request_uri");
                if(requestPath == null) {
                        requestPath = request.getRequestURI();
                }
                errorDetail.setTitle("Validation Failed");
                errorDetail.setDetail("Input validation failed");
                errorDetail.setDeveloperMessage(manve.getClass().
                getName());

                // Create ValidationError instances
                List<FieldError> fieldErrors =  manve.getBindingResult().
                getFieldErrors();
                for(FieldError fe : fieldErrors) {

List<ValidationError> validationErrorList = errorDetail.getErrors().get
(fe.getField());
                        if(validationErrorList == null) {
                                validationErrorList = new
                                ArrayList<ValidationError>();
```

```
errorDetail.getErrors().put(fe.getField(), validationErrorList);
                    }
                    ValidationError validationError = new
                    ValidationError();
                    validationError.setCode(fe.getCode());
                    validationError.setMessage(fe.getDefaultMessage());
                    validationErrorList.add(validationError);
            }

            return new ResponseEntity<>(errorDetail, null, HttpStatus.
            BAD_REQUEST);
                }

        /** handleResourceNotFoundException method removed **/

}
```

With this implementation in place, restart the QuickPoll application and submit a Poll with missing question. This will result in a status code of 400 with our custom error response, as shown in Figure 5-9.

Figure 5-9. *Validation error response*

Externalizing Error Messages

We have made quite a bit of progress with our input validation and provided the client with descriptive error messages that can help them troubleshoot and recover from those errors. However, the actual validation error message may not be very descriptive and API developers might want to change it. It would be even better if they were able to pull this message from an external properties file. The property file approach not only simplifies Java code but also makes it easy to swap the messages without making code changes.

It also sets the stage for future internationalization/localization needs. To achieve this, create a messages.properties file under the src\main\resources folder, and add the following two messages:

```
NotEmpty.poll.question=Question is a required field
Size.poll.options=Options must be greater than {2} and less than {1}
```

As you can see, we are following the convention <<Constraint_Name>>.model_name. field_Name for each key of the message. The model_name represents name of the Spring MVC's model object to which user-submitted data is being bound. The name is typically provided using the @ModelAttribute annotation. In the scenarios in which this annotation is missing, the model name is derived using the parameter's nonqualified class name. The PollController's createPoll method takes a com.apress.domain. Poll instance as its model object. Hence, in this case, the model name will be derived as *poll*. If a controller were to take an instance of com.apress.domain.SomeObject as its parameter, the derived model name will be *someObject*. It is important to remember that Spring will not use the name of the method parameter as the model name.

The next step is to read the properties from the file and use them during the ValidationError instance creation. We do that by injecting an instance of MessageSource into the RestExceptionHandler class. Spring's MessageSource provides an abstraction to easily resolve messages. Listing 5-12 shows the modified source code for handleValidationError. Notice that we are using MessageResource's getMessage method to retrieve messages.

Listing 5-12. Reading Messages from Properties File

```
@ControllerAdvice
public class RestExceptionHandler {

        @Inject
        private MessageSource messageSource;

        @ExceptionHandler(MethodArgumentNotValidException.class)
        @ResponseStatus(HttpStatus.BAD_REQUEST)

public @ResponseBody ErrorDetail handleValidationError(MethodArgumentNot
ValidException manve, HttpServletRequest request) {

            ErrorDetail errorDetail = new ErrorDetail();
            // Populate errorDetail instance
```

```
                errorDetail.setTimeStamp(new Date().getTime());
                errorDetail.setStatus(HttpStatus.BAD_REQUEST.value());

String requestPath = (String) request.getAttribute("javax.servlet.error.
request_uri");
                if(requestPath == null) {
                        requestPath = request.getRequestURI();
                }
                errorDetail.setTitle("Validation Failed");
                errorDetail.setDetail("Input validation failed");
                errorDetail.setDeveloperMessage(manve.getClass().
                getName());

                // Create ValidationError instances
                List<FieldError> fieldErrors =  manve.getBindingResult().
                getFieldErrors();
                for(FieldError fe : fieldErrors) {

List<ValidationError> validationErrorList = errorDetail.getErrors().get
(fe.getField());
                        if(validationErrorList == null) {
                                validationErrorList = new ArrayList
                                <ValidationError>();

errorDetail.getErrors().put(fe.getField(), validationErrorList);
                        }
                        ValidationError validationError = new
                        ValidationError();
                        validationError.setCode(fe.getCode());
                        validationError.setMessage(messageSource.
                        getMessage(fe, null));
                        validationErrorList.add(validationError);
                }

                return errorDetail;
        }
}
```

Restarting the QuickPoll application and submitting a poll with a missing question would result in the new validation error message as shown in Figure 5-10.

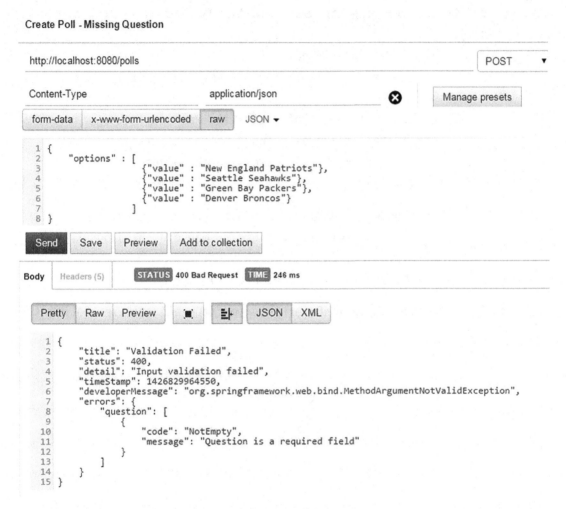

Figure 5-10. *New validation error message*

Improving RestExceptionHandler

By default, Spring MVC handles error scenarios such as not being able to read a malformed request or not finding a required request parameter by throwing a set of standard exceptions. However, Spring MVC doesn't write these standard exception details to the response body. To keep things consistent for our QuickPoll clients, it is important that Spring MVC standard exceptions are also handled in the same way and that we return the same error response format. A straightforward approach is to create a handler method for each exception in our RestExceptionHandler. A simpler approach is to have RestExceptionHandler class extend Spring's ResponseEntityExceptionHandler. The ResponseEntityExceptionHandler class contains a set of protected methods that handle standard exception and return a ResponseEntity instance containing error details.

Extending the ResponseEntityExceptionHandler class allows us to override the protected method associated with the exception and return an ErrorDetail instance. Listing 5-13 shows a modified RestExceptionHandler that overrides handleHttpMessageNotReadable method. The method implementation follows the same pattern that we used before—create and populate an instance of ErrorDetail. Because the ResponseEntityExceptionHandler already comes with a handler method for MethodArgumentNotValidException, we have moved the handleValidationError method code to an overridden handleMethodArgumentNotValid method.

Listing 5-13. RestExceptionHandler Handling Malformed Messages

```
@ControllerAdvice
public class RestExceptionHandler extends ResponseEntityExceptionHandler  {

        @Override
        protected ResponseEntity<Object> handleHttpMessageNotReadable(
                    HttpMessageNotReadableException ex, HttpHeaders
                    headers,
                    HttpStatus status, WebRequest request) {

            ErrorDetail errorDetail = new ErrorDetail();
            errorDetail.setTimeStamp(new Date().getTime());
            errorDetail.setStatus(status.value());
            errorDetail.setTitle("Message Not Readable");
            errorDetail.setDetail(ex.getMessage());
            errorDetail.setDeveloperMessage(ex.getClass().getName());

            return handleExceptionInternal(ex, errorDetail, headers,
            status, request);
        }
        @Override
```

```
public ResponseEntity<Object> handleMethodArgumentNotValid(MethodArgumentNot
ValidException manve, HttpHeaders headers, HttpStatus status, WebRequest
request) {

                // implementation removed for brevity

            return handleExceptionInternal(manve, errorDetail, headers,
            status, request);
    }
}
```

Let's quickly verify our implementation by submitting a nonreadable message (such as removing a "," from the JSON request body) using Postman. You should see a response as shown in Figure 5-11.

Figure 5-11. *Not Readable message error*

Summary

In this chapter, we designed and implemented an error response format for Spring MVC–based REST applications. We also looked at validating user input and returning error messages that are meaningful to API consumers. In the next chapter, we will look at strategies for documenting REST services using the Swagger framework.

CHAPTER 6

Documenting REST Services

In this chapter we will discuss the following:

- The basics of Swagger

- Using Swagger for API documentation

- Customizing Swagger

Documentation is an important aspect of any project. This is especially true for enterprise and open-source projects, where many people collaborate to build the project. In this chapter, we will look at Swagger, a tool that simplifies REST API documentation.

Documenting a REST API for consumers to use and interact with is a difficult task because there are no real established standards. Organizations have historically relied on manually edited documents to expose REST contracts to clients. With SOAP-based web services, a WSDL serves as a contract for the client and provides a detailed description of the operations and associated request/response payloads. The WADL, or Web Application Description Language, specification tried to fill this gap in the REST web services world, but it didn't get a lot of adoption. In recent years, there has been growth in the number of metadata standards such as Swagger, Apiary, and iODocs for describing REST services. Most of them grew out of the need to document APIs, thereby expanding an API's adoption.

© Balaji Varanasi and Maxim Bartkov 2022
B. Varanasi and M. Bartkov, *Spring REST*, https://doi.org/10.1007/978-1-4842-7477-4_6

Swagger

Swagger (http://swagger.io) is a specification and a framework for creating interactive REST API documentation. It enables documentation to be in sync with any changes made to REST services. It also provides a set of tools and SDK generators for generating API client code. Swagger was originally developed by Wordnik in early 2010 and is currently backed by SmartBear software.

Swagger is a language-agnostic specification with implementations available for a variety of languages such as Java, Scala, and PHP. A full description of specifications can be found at https://github.com/springfox/springfox. The specification is made up of two file types—a resource listing file and a set of API declaration files that describe the REST API and the available operations.

The resource listing file referred to by the name "api-docs" is the root document for describing the API. It contains general information about the API such as the API version, title, description, and license. As the name suggests, the resource listing file also contains all of the API resources available in the application. Listing 6-1 shows a sample resource listing file for a hypothetical REST API. Notice that Swagger uses JSON as its description language. From the APIs array in Listing 6-1, you can see that the resource listing file has two API resources declared, namely, products and orders. The URIs /default/products and /default/orders allow you to access the resource's API declaration file. Swagger allows grouping of its resources; by default, all resources are grouped under the default group and, hence, the "/default" in the URI. The info object contains the contact and licensing information associated with the API.

Listing 6-1. Sample Resource File

```
{
    "apiVersion": "1.0",
    "swaggerVersion": "1.2"
    "apis": [
                {
                        "description": "Endpoint for Product management",
                        "path": "/default/products"
                },
                {
                        "description": "Endpoint for Order management",
```

```
                    "path": "/default/orders"
                }
        ],
        "authorizations": { },
        "info" : {
        "contact": "contact@test.com",
        "description": "Api for an ecommerce application",
        "license": "Apache 2.0",
        "licenseUrl": "http://www.apache.org/licenses/LICENSE-2.0.html",
        "termsOfServiceUrl": "Api terms of service",
        "title": "ECommerce App"
    }
}
```

An API declaration file describes a resource along with the API operations and request/response representations. Listing 6-2 shows a sample API declaration file for the product resource and will be served at the URI /default/products. The basePath field provides the Root URI serving the API. The resourcePath specifies the resource path relative to the basePath. In this case, we are specifying that the product's REST API is accessible at http://server:port/products. The APIs field contains API objects that describe an API operation. Listing 6-2 describes one API operation called createProduct and its associated HTTP method, the media type of the messages consumed/produced, and API responses. The models field contains any model objects associated with the resource. Listing 6-2 shows a product model object associated with a product resource.

Listing 6-2. Sample Products API Declaration File at /default/products

```
{
    "apiVersion": "1.0",
    "swaggerVersion": "1.2"
    "basePath": "/",
    "resourcePath": "/products",
    "apis": [
            {
                "description": "createProduct",
                "operations": [
```

```
{
        "method": "POST",
        "produces": [ "application/json" ],
        "consumes": [ "application/json" ],
        "parameters": [ { "allowMultiple": false} ],
            "responseMessages": [
            {
                "code": 200,
                "message": null,
                "responseModel": "object"
            }
            ]
        }
        ],
        "path": "/products"
    }
    ],
    "models": {
        "Product": {
        "description": "",
        "id": "Product",
        "properties": { }
        }
    }
}
```

Note   In our hypothetical example, Swagger expects the API declaration file for the product resource to reside at the "/default/products" URI. This should not be confused with the actual REST API location for accessing the product resource. In this example, the declaration file indicates that the product resource is accessible at http://server:port/products URI.

Integrating Swagger

Integrating Swagger involves creating the "api-docs" resource listing file and a set of API declaration files describing API's resources. Instead of hand-coding these files, there are several Swagger and community-owned projects that integrate with existing source code and automatically generate these files. springfox-boot-starter is one such framework that simplifies Swagger integration with Spring MVC–based projects. We begin the Swagger integration with QuickPoll application by adding the springfox-boot-starter Maven dependency shown in Listing 6-3 in the pom.xml file.

Note   We continue our tradition of building on the work we did on the QuickPoll application in the previous chapters. You can also use the starter project available at Chapter6\starter folder of the downloaded source code. The completed solution is available under the Chapter6\final folder.

Listing 6-3. Springfox-Boot-Starter Dependency

```
<dependency>
    <groupId>io.springfox</groupId>
    <artifactId>springfox-boot-starter</artifactId>
    <version>3.0.0</version>
</dependency>
```

By the next step, we have to define bean Docket as shown in Listing 6-4.

Listing 6-4. Define Docket Bean

```
import org.springframework.context.annotation.Bean;
import org.springframework.context.annotation.Configuration;
import org.springframework.web.servlet.config.annotation.
ResourceHandlerRegistry;
import org.springframework.web.servlet.config.annotation.
WebMvcConfigurerAdapter;
import springfox.documentation.builders.PathSelectors;
```

```
import springfox.documentation.builders.RequestHandlerSelectors;
import springfox.documentation.spi.DocumentationType;
import springfox.documentation.spring.web.plugins.Docket;

@Configuration
public class SwaggerConfiguration {

    @Bean
    public Docket api() {
        return new Docket(DocumentationType.SWAGGER_2)
                .select()
                .paths(PathSelectors.any())
                .build();
    }
}
```

With this minimal configuration in place, run the QuickPoll application and launch the URI http://localhost:8080/v3/api-docs. You should see the resource listing file as shown in Figure 6-1.

```
{
    apiVersion: "1.0",
  ▾ apis: [
     ▾ {
            description: "Basic Error Controller",
            path: "/default/basic-error-controller",
            position: 0
        },
     ▾ {
            description: "Compute Result Controller",
            path: "/default/compute-result-controller",
            position: 0
        },
     ▾ {
            description: "Poll Controller",
            path: "/default/poll-controller",
            position: 0
        },
     ▾ {
            description: "Vote Controller",
            path: "/default/vote-controller",
            position: 0
        }
    ],
    authorizations: { },
  ▾ info: {
        contact: "Contact Email",
        description: "Api Description",
        license: "Licence Type",
        licenseUrl: "License URL",
        termsOfServiceUrl: "Api terms of service",
        title: "default Title"
    },
    swaggerVersion: "1.2"
}
```

Figure 6-1. *QuickPoll resource listing file*

Swagger UI

The resource listing and API declaration files act as valuable resources for understanding
a REST API. Swagger UI is a subproject of Swagger that takes these files and
automatically generates a pleasant, intuitive interface for interacting with API. Using this
interface, both technical and nontechnical folks can test REST services by submitting
requests and see how those services respond. The Swagger UI is built using HTML, CSS,
and JavaScript and doesn't have any other external dependencies. It can be hosted in any
server environment or can even run from your local machine.

The springfox-boot-starter already included work with Swagger UI that uses JSON from `http://localhost:8080/v3/api-docs` and parsing JSON in readable UI as shown in Figure 6-2.

Without some modifications, we are ready to launch Swagger UI. Run the quick-poll application and navigate to the URL `http://localhost:8080/swagger-ui.html`. You should see QuickPoll Swagger UI, as shown in Figure 6-2.

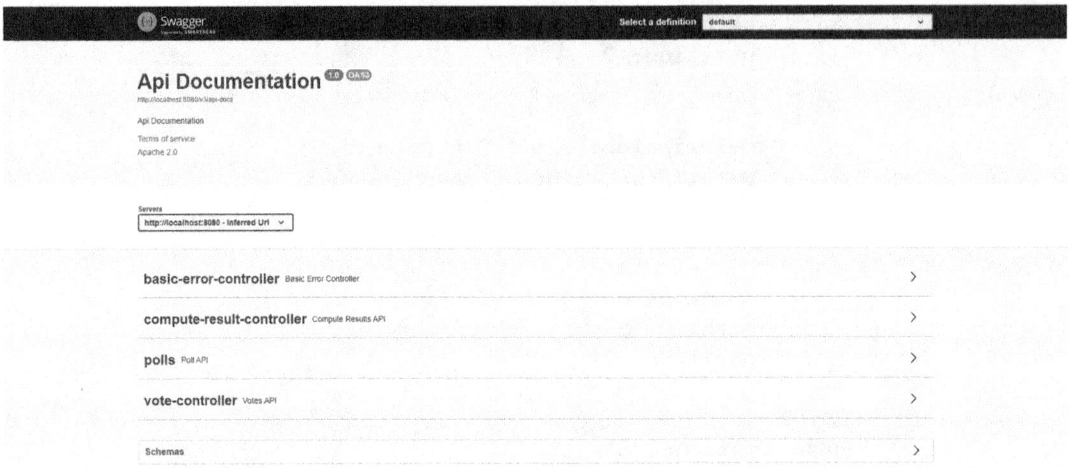

Figure 6-2. *QuickPoll Swagger UI*

Using the UI, you should be able to perform operations such as creating polls and reading all polls.

Customizing Swagger

In the previous sections, you have seen that with minimal configuration, we were able to create interactive documentation using Swagger. Additionally, this documentation would automatically update itself when we make changes to our services. However, you will notice that out of the box, the title and the API descriptions are not very intuitive. Also, the URLs such as "Terms of Service," "Contact the Developer," and so on don't work. As you explore the UI, the Response classes such as Poll and Vote are not visible in the Swagger UI, and the user has to end up guessing what the return type for the operations is going to be.

Swagger Springfox provides a convenient builder named Docket for customizing and configuring Swagger. The Docket provides convenient methods and sensible defaults but itself uses the ApiInfo class to perform the actual configuration. We begin our Swagger customization by creating a SwaggerConfig class under the com.apress package in our QuickPoll application. Populate the newly created class with the contents of Listing 6-5.

Listing 6-5. Custom Swagger Implementation

```
package com.apress;

import org.springframework.context.annotation.Bean;
import org.springframework.context.annotation.Configuration;
import org.springframework.web.servlet.config.annotation.
ResourceHandlerRegistry;
import org.springframework.web.servlet.config.annotation.
WebMvcConfigurerAdapter;
import springfox.documentation.builders.PathSelectors;
import springfox.documentation.builders.RequestHandlerSelectors;
import springfox.documentation.service.ApiInfo;
import springfox.documentation.service.Contact;
import springfox.documentation.spi.DocumentationType;
import springfox.documentation.spring.web.plugins.Docket;
import java.util.Collections;

@Configuration
public class SwaggerConfiguration {

    @Bean
    public Docket api() {
        return new Docket(DocumentationType.SWAGGER_2)
                .select()
                .apis(RequestHandlerSelectors.basePackage("com.apress.
                controller"))
                .paths(PathSelectors.any())
                .build()
                .apiInfo(apiInfo());
    }
```

```
private ApiInfo apiInfo() {
    return new ApiInfo(
            "QuickPoll REST API",
            "QuickPoll Api for creating and managing polls",
            "http://example.com/terms-of-service",
            "Terms of service",
            new Contact("Maxim Bartkov", "www.example.com", "info@
            example.com"),
            "MIT License", "http://opensource.org/licenses/MIT",
            Collections.emptyList());
    }
}
```

The SwaggerConfig class is annotated with @Configuration indicating that it contains one or more Spring bean configurations. Because the Docket relies on the framework's SpringSwaggerConfig, we inject an instance of SpringSwaggerConfig for later use. The SpringSwaggerConfig is a Spring-managed bean that gets instantiated during Spring's component scanning in JAR files.

The configureSwagger method contains the meat of our Swagger configuration. The method is annotated with @Bean, indicating to Spring that the return value is a Spring bean and needs to be registered within a BeanFactory. The Swagger Springfox framework picks up this bean and customizes Swagger. We begin the method implementation by creating an instance of SwaggerSpringMvcPlugin. Then, using the ApiInfoBuilder, we create an ApiInfo object containing the title, description, contact, and license information associated with the QuickPoll application. Finally, we pass the created apiInfo and apiVersion information to the Docket instance and return it.

Note   It is possible to have multiple methods producing Docket beans. Each Docket would result in a separate resource listing. This is useful in situations in which you have the same Spring MVC application that serves more than one API or multiple versions of the same API.

With the new SwaggerConfig class added, run the QuickPoll application and navigate to http://localhost:8080/swagger-ui.html. You will see the changes reflected in our UI as shown in Figure 6-3.

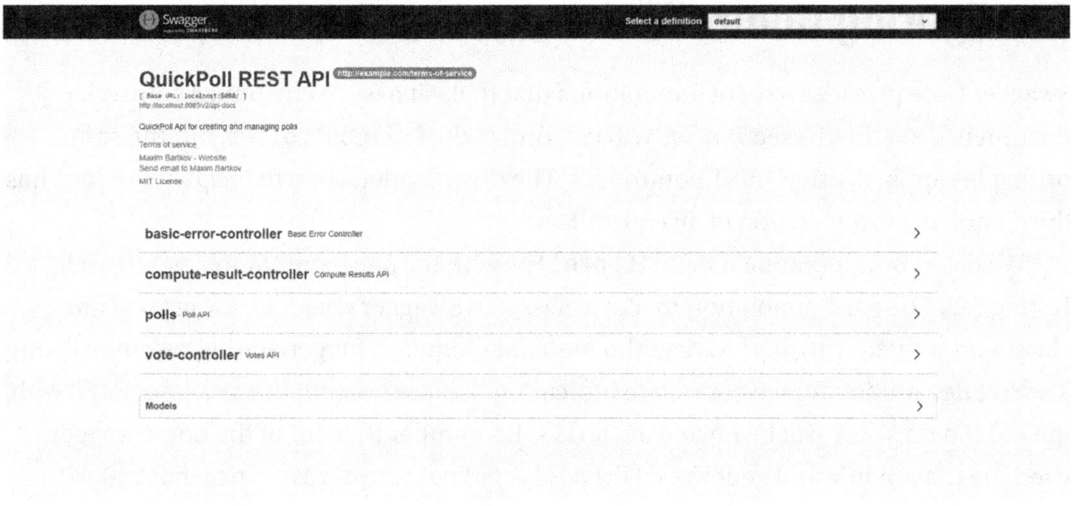

Figure 6-3. *Updated QuickPoll Swagger UI*

From Figure 6-3, you will notice that in addition to the three QuickPoll REST endpoints, there is a Spring Boot's "/error" endpoint. Because this endpoint really doesn't serve any purpose, let's hide it from our API documentation. To accomplish this, we will use the Docket class's handy includePattern method. The includePattern method allows us to specify which request mappings should be included in the resource listing. Listing 6-6 shows the updated portion of the SwaggerConfig's configureSwagger method. The paths method by default takes regular expressions, and, in our case, we explicitly listed all three endpoints we would like to include.

Listing 6-6. ConfigureSwagger Method with IncludePatterns

```
docket
            .apiInfo(apiInfo)
            .paths(PathSelectors.regex("/polls/*.*|/votes/*.*|/
            computeresult/*.*"));
```

Rerun the QuickPoll application and you will see the Spring Boot's error controller no longer appearing in the documentation.

Configuring Controllers

Swagger Core provides a set of annotations that make it easy to customize controller documentation. In this section, we will customize the PollController, but the same principles apply to other REST controllers. The downloaded code in Chapter6\final has the complete customization of all controllers.

We begin by annotating the PollContoller with the @Api annotation as shown in Listing 6-7. The @Api annotation marks a class as a Swagger resource. Swagger scans classes annotated with @Api to read the metadata required for generating resource listing and API declaration files. Here we are indicating that the documentation associated with the PollController will be hosted at /polls. Remember that out of the box, Swagger used the Class name and generated URI poll-controller (http://localhost:8080/swagger-ui/index.html#!/poll-controller) to host the documentation. With our change, the PollController Swagger documentation is accessible at http://localhost:8080/swagger-ui.html#!/polls. Using the @Api annotation, we have also provided the description associated with our Poll API.

Listing 6-7. @Api Annotation in Action

```
import io.swagger.annotations.Api;

@RestController
@Api(value = "polls", description = "Poll API")
public class PollController {
        // Implementation removed for brevity
}
```

Run the QuickPoll application, and, on navigating to Swagger UI at http://localhost:8080/swagger-ui/index.html, you will notice the updated URI path and description as shown in Figure 6-4.

---

polls : Poll API   Show/Hide | List Operations

Figure 6-4. *Updated poll endpoint*

Now we will move on to the API operation customization using the @ApiOperation annotation. This annotation allows us to customize the operation information such as name, description, and response. Listing 6-8 shows the @ApiOperation applied to the createPoll, getPoll, and getAllPolls methods. We use the value attribute to provide a brief description of the operation. Swagger recommends limiting this field to 120 characters. The notes field can be used to provide more descriptive information about the operation.

Listing 6-8. @ApiOperation Annotated Methods

```
import io.swagger.annotations.ApiOperation;

@ApiOperation(value = "Creates a new Poll", notes="The newly created poll
Id will be sent in the location response header", response = Void.class)
@PostMapping("/polls")
public ResponseEntity<Void> createPoll(@Valid @RequestBody Poll poll) {
        ........
}

@ApiOperation(value = "Retrieves a Poll associated with the pollId",
response=Poll.class)
@GetMapping("/polls/{pollId}")
public ResponseEntity<?> getPoll(@PathVariable Long pollId) {
        .........
}

@ApiOperation(value = "Retrieves all the polls", response=Poll.class,
responseContainer="List")
@GetMapping("/polls")
public ResponseEntity<Iterable<Poll>> getAllPolls() {
        ..........
}
```

The createPoll method on successful completion sends an empty body and a status code 201 to the client. However, because we are returning a ResponseEntity, Swagger is not able to figure out the right response model. We fix this using ApiOperation's response attribute and setting it to a Void.class. We also changed the method return type from ResponseEntity<?> to ResponseEntity<Void> to make our intent more clear.

The getPoll method returns a poll associated with the passed in pollId parameter. Hence, we set the ApiOperation's response attribute to Poll.class. Because the getAllPolls method returns a collection of Poll instances, we have used the responseContainer attribute and set its value to List.

With these annotations added, rerun and launch QuickPoll application's Swagger UI to verify that the descriptions, response model, and notes sections are changed. For example, click the "polls" link next to "Poll API" to expand the PollController's operations. Then click the "/polls/{pollId}" link next to GET to see the response model associated with getPoll method. Figure 6-5 shows this updated response model.

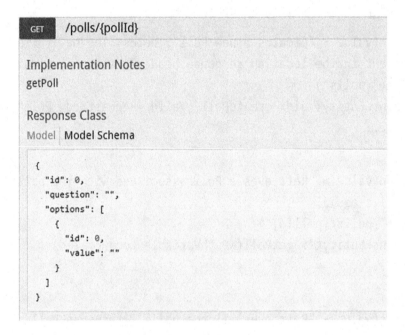

Figure 6-5. *GetPoll method's updated model*

The @ApiOperation we used earlier allows us to specify an operation's default return type. As we have seen throughout the book, a well-defined API uses additional status codes, and Swagger provides the @ApiResponse annotation to configure the codes and associated response body. Listing 6-9 shows the createPoll method annotated with @ApiResponse for status codes 201 and 500. Swagger requires us to place all the @ApiResponse annotations inside a wrapper @ApiResponse annotation. With the status code 201, we have added notes indicating how to retrieve the newly created poll ID. With the status code 500, we have indicated that the response body will contain an ErrorDetail instance.

Listing 6-9. @ApiResponse Annotations

```java
import com.wordnik.swagger.annotations.ApiResponse;
import com.wordnik.swagger.annotations.ApiResponses;

        @ApiOperation(value = "Creates a new Poll", notes="The newly
        created poll Id will be sent in the location response header",
        response = Void.class)
        @ApiResponses(value = {@ApiResponse(code=201, message="Poll Created
        Successfully", response=Void.class),
                        @ApiResponse(code=500, message="Error creating
                        Poll", response=ErrorDetail.class) } )
    @PostMapping("/polls")
    public ResponseEntity<Void> createPoll(@Valid @RequestBody Poll
    poll) {
    // Content removed for brevity
}
```

Run the QuickPoll application and navigate to Swagger UI. Click the "polls" link next to "Poll API" to expand the PollController's operations. Then click the "/polls" link next to POST to see the updated notes and `ErrorDetail` model schema. Figure 6-6 shows the expected output.

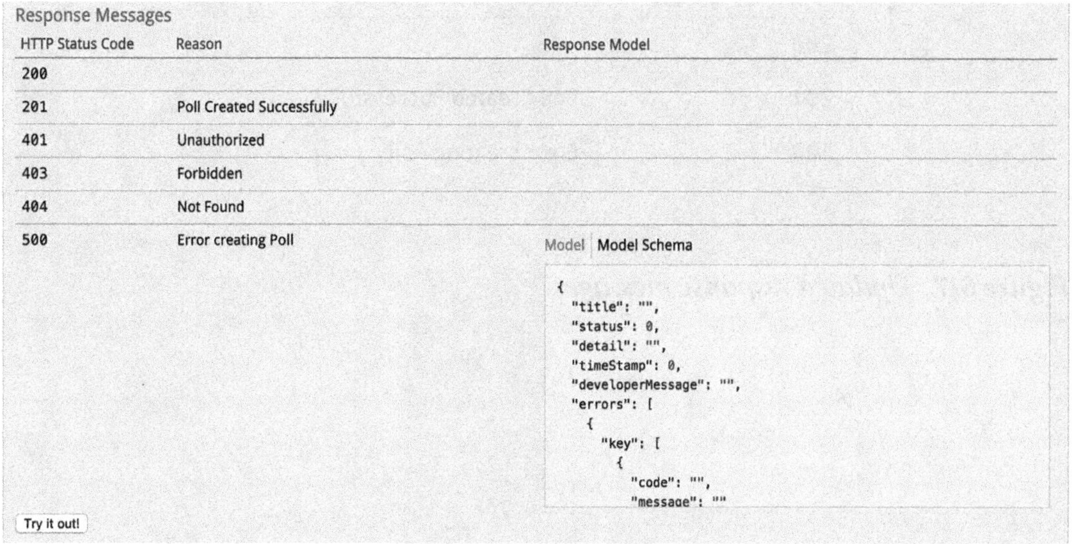

Figure 6-6. *Modified response messages*

A quick glance at Figure 6-6 shows that we have more response than configured messages. This is because Swagger out of the box adds a set of default response messages for each HTTP method. This behavior can be disabled using the useDefaultResponseMessages method in the Docket class as shown in Listing 6-10.

Listing 6-10. Ignore Default Response Messages

```
public class SwaggerConfig {

        @Bean
        public Docket configureSwagger() {
            // Content removed

            docket.useDefaultResponseMessages(false);
            return docket;
        }
}
```

Run the QuickPoll application and repeat these steps to view the response messages associated with the POST operation on "/polls" URI. As shown in Figure 6-7, the default response messages are no longer displayed.

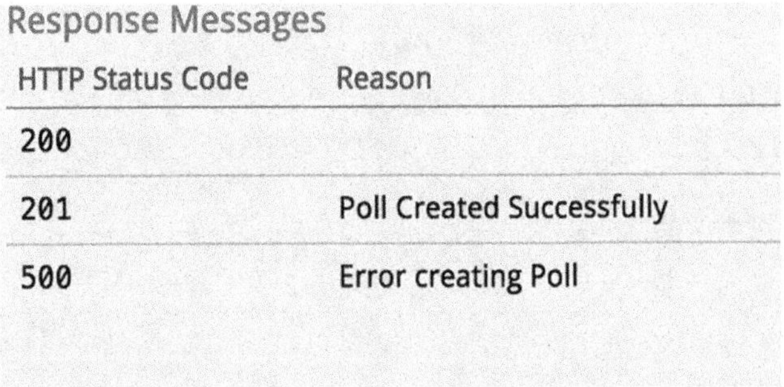

Response Messages	
HTTP Status Code	Reason
200	
201	Poll Created Successfully
500	Error creating Poll

Figure 6-7. *Updated response messages*

In addition to the configuration options we looked at, Swagger provides the following annotations to configure model objects:

- `@ApiModel`—Annotation that allows changing the name of the model or providing a description to the associated model

- `@ApiModelProperty`—Annotation that can be used to provide property description and list of allowed values and to indicate if it is required or not

Summary

Documentation plays an important role in understanding and consuming a REST API. In this chapter, we reviewed the basics of Swagger and integrated it with a QuickPoll application to generate interactive documentation. We also looked at customizing Swagger to meet our application-specific needs.

In the next chapter, we will look at techniques for versioning REST API and implementing paging and sorting capabilities.

CHAPTER 7

Versioning, Paging, and Sorting

In this chapter we will discuss the following:

- Strategies for versioning REST services
- Adding pagination capabilities
- Adding sorting capabilities

We all are familiar with the famous proverb "The only thing constant in life is change." This applies to software development. In this chapter, we will look at versioning our API as a way to handle such changes. Additionally, dealing with large datasets can be problematic especially when mobile clients are involved. Large datasets can also result in server overload and performance issues. To handle this, we will employ paging and sorting techniques and send data in manageable chunks.

Versioning

As user requirements and technology change, no matter how planned our design is, we will end up changing our code. This will involve making changes to REST resources by adding, updating, and sometimes removing attributes. Although the crux of the API—read, create, update, and remove one or more resources—remains the same, this could result in such drastic changes to the representation that it may break any existing consumers. Similarly, changes to functionality such as securing our services and requiring authentication or authorization can break existing consumers. Such major changes typically call for new versions of the API.

147

© Balaji Varanasi and Maxim Bartkov 2022
B. Varanasi and M. Bartkov, *Spring REST*, https://doi.org/10.1007/978-1-4842-7477-4_7

In this chapter, we will be adding paging and sorting functionality to our QuickPoll API. As you will see in later sections, this change will result in changes to the representations returned for some of the GET HTTP methods. Before we version our QuickPoll API to handle paging and sorting, let's look at some approaches for versioning.

Versioning Approaches

There are four popular approaches to versioning a REST API:

- URI versioning

- URI parameter versioning

- Accept header versioning

- Custom header versioning

None of these approaches are silver bullets, and each has its fair share of advantages and disadvantages. In this section we will look at these approaches along with some real-world public APIs that use them.

URI Versioning

In this approach, version information becomes part of the URI. For example, `http://api.example.org/v1/users` and `http://api.example.org/v2/users` represent two different versions of an application API. Here we use `v` notation to denote versioning, and the numbers 1 and 2 following the `v` indicate the first and second API versions.

URI versioning has been one of the most commonly used approaches and is used by major public APIs such as Twitter, LinkedIn, Yahoo, and SalesForce. Here are some examples:

- LinkedIn: `https://api.linkedin.com/v1/people/~`

- Yahoo: `https://social.yahooapis.com/v1/user/12345/profile`

- SalesForce: `http://na1.salesforce.com/services/data/v26.0`

- Twitter: `https://api.twitter.com/1.1/statuses/user_timeline.json`

- Twilio: `https://api.twilio.com/2010-04-01/Accounts/{AccountSid}/Calls`

As you can see, LinkedIn, Yahoo, and SalesForce use the v notation. In addition to a major version, SalesForce uses a minor version as part of its URI version. Twilio, by contrast, takes a unique approach and uses a timestamp in the URI to differentiate its versions.

Making a version part of the URI is very appealing as the version information is right in the URI. It also simplifies API development and testing. Folks can easily browse and use different versions of REST services via a web browser. On the contrary, this might make client's life difficult. For example, consider a client storing references to user resources in its database. On switching to a new version, these references get outdated and the client has to do a mass database update to upgrade references to new version.

URI Parameter Versioning

This is similar to the URI versioning that we just looked at except that the version information is specified as a URI request parameter. For example, the URI `http://api.example.org/users?v=2` uses the version parameter v to represent the second version of the API. The version parameter is typically optional, and a default version of the API will continue working for requests without version parameter. Most often, the default version is the latest version of the API.

Although as not popular as other versioning strategies, a few major public APIs such as Netflix have used this strategy. The URI parameter versioning shares the same disadvantages of URI versioning. Another disadvantage is that some proxies don't cache resources with a URI parameter, resulting in additional network traffic.

Accept Header Versioning

This versioning approach uses the `Accept` header to communicate version information. Because the header contains version information, there will be only one URI for multiple versions of API.

Up to this point, we have used standard media types such as `"application/json"` as part of the `Accept` header to indicate the type of content the client expects. To pass additional version information, we need a custom media type. The following convention is popular when creating a custom media type:

```
vnd.product_name.version+ suffix
```

The vnd is the starting point of the custom media type and indicates vendor. The product or producer name is the name of the product and distinguishes this media type from other custom product media types. The version part is represented using strings such as v1 or v2 or v3. Finally, the suffix is used to specify the structure of the media type. For example, the +json suffix indicates a structure that follows the guidelines established for media type "application/json." RFC 6389 (https://tools.ietf.org/html/rfc6839) gives a full list of standardized prefixes such as +xml, +json, and +zip. Using this approach, a client, for example, can send an application/vnd.quickpoll.v2+json accept header to request the second version of the API.

The Accept header versioning approach is becoming more and more popular as it allows fine-grained versioning of individual resources without impacting the entire API. This approach can make browser testing harder as we have to carefully craft the Accept header. GitHub is a popular public API that uses this Accept header strategy. For requests that don't contain any Accept header, GitHub uses the latest version of the API to fulfill the request.

Custom Header Versioning

The custom header versioning approach is similar to the Accept header versioning approach except that instead of the Accept header, a custom header is used. Microsoft Azure takes this approach and uses the custom header x-ms-version. For example, to get the latest version of Azure at the time of writing this book, your request needs to include a custom header:

```
x-ms-version: 2021-09-14
```

This approach shares the same pros and cons as that of the Accept header approach. Because the HTTP specification provides a standard way of accomplishing this via the Accept header, the custom header approach hasn't been widely adopted.

Deprecating an API

As you release new versions of an API, maintaining older versions becomes cumbersome and can result in maintenance nightmares. The number of versions to maintain and their longevity depend on the API user base, but it is strongly recommended to maintain at least one older version.

API versions that will no longer be maintained need to be deprecated and eventually retired. It is important to remember that deprecation is intended to communicate that the API is still available but will cease to exist in the future. API users should be given plenty of notices about deprecation so that they can migrate to newer versions.

QuickPoll Versioning

In this book, we will be using the URI versioning approach to version the QuickPoll REST API.

Implementing and maintaining different versions of an API can be difficult, as it generally complicates code. We want to make sure that changes in one version of code don't impact other versions of the code. To improve maintainability, we want to make sure that we avoid code duplication as much as possible. Here are two approaches for organizing code to support multiple API versions:

- Complete code replication—In this approach, you replicate the entire code base and maintain parallel code paths for each version. Popular API builder Apigility takes this approach and clones the entire code base for each new version. This approach makes it easy to make code changes that wouldn't impact other versions. It also makes it easy to switch backend datastores. This would also allow each version to become a separate deployable artifact. Although this approach provides a lot of flexibility, we will be duplicating the entire code base.

- Version-specific code replication—In this approach, we only replicate the code that is specific to each version. Each version can have its own set of controllers and request/response DTO objects but will reuse most of the common service and backend layers. For smaller applications, this approach can work well as version-specific code can simply be separated into different packages. Care must be taken when making changes to the reused code, as it might have impact on multiple versions.

Spring MVC makes it easy to version a QuickPoll application using the URI versioning approach. Considering that versioning plays a crucial role in managing changes, it is important that we version as early as possible in the development cycle. Hence, we will assign a version (v1) to all of the QuickPoll services that we have developed so far. To support multiple versions, we will follow the second approach and create a separate set of controllers.

Note   In this chapter we will continue building on the work that we did on the QuickPoll application in the previous chapters. Alternatively, a starter project inside the `Chapter7\starter` folder of the downloaded source code is available for you to use. The completed solution is available under the `Chapter7\final` folder. Please refer to this solution for complete listings containing getters/setters and additional imports. The downloaded `Chapter7` folder also contains an exported Postman collection containing REST API requests associated with this chapter.

We begin the versioning process by creating two packages `com.apress.v1.controller` and `com.apress.v2.controller`. Move all of the controllers from the `com.apress.controller` package to the `com.apress.v1.controller`. To each controller in the new v1 package, add a class-level `@RequestMapping ("/v1")` annotation. Because we will have multiple versions of controllers, we need to give unique component names to individual controllers. We will follow the convention of appending version number to the *unqualified* class name to derive our component name. Using this convention, the v1 `PollController` will have a component name `pollControllerV1`.

Listing 7-1 shows the portion of the `PollController` class with these modifications. Notice that the component name is provided as a value to the `@RestController` annotation. Similarly, assign the component name voteControllerV1 to the v1 `VoteController` and computeResultControllerV1 to the v1 `ComputeResultController`.

Listing 7-1. Version 1 of the Poll Controller

```
package com.apress.v1.controller;

import org.springframework.web.bind.annotation.RequestMapping;

@RestController("pollControllerV1")
@RequestMapping("/v1")
@Api(value = "polls", description = "Poll API")
public class PollController {

}
```

Note   Even though the behavior and code of VoteController and ComputeResultControler don't change across versions, we are copying the code to keep things simple. In real-world scenarios, refactor code into reusable modules, or use inheritance to avoid code duplication.

With the class-level @RequestMapping annotation in place, all of the URIs in the v1 PollController become relative to "/v1/." Restart the QuickPoll application, and, using Postman, verify that you can create a new Poll at the new http://localhost:8080/v1/polls endpoint.

To create the second version of the API, copy all of the controllers from the v1 package to the v2 package. Change the class-level RequestMapping value from "/v1/" to "/v2/" and the component name suffix from "V1" to "V2." Listing 7-2 shows the modified portions of the V2 version of the PollController. Because the v2 PollController is a copy of the v1 PollController, we have omitted the PollController class implementation from Listing 7-2.

Listing 7-2. Version 2 of the Poll Controller

```
@RestController("pollControllerV2")
@RequestMapping("/v2")
@Api(value = "polls", description = "Poll API")
public class PollController {
        // Code copied from the v1 Poll Controller
}
```

Once you have completed modifications for the three controllers, restart the QuickPoll application, and, using Postman, verify that you can create a new poll using the http://localhost:8080/v2/polls endpoint. Similarly, verify that you can access the VoteController and ComputeResultController endpoints by accessing the http://localhost:8080/v2/votes and http://localhost:8080/v2/computeresult endpoints.

SwaggerConfig

The versioning changes that we made require changes to our Swagger configuration so that we can use the UI to test and interact with both REST API versions. Listing 7-3 shows the refactored com.apress.SwaggerConfig class. As discussed in the previous chapter, a springfox.documentation.spring.web.plugins.Docket instance represents a Swagger group. Hence, the refactored SwaggerConfig class contains two methods, each returning a Docket instance representing an API group. Also, notice that we have extracted API information to its own method and used it to configure both instances of Docket.

Listing 7-3. Refactored SwaggerConfig Class

```
package com.apress;
import org.springframework.context.annotation.Bean;
import org.springframework.context.annotation.Configuration;
import springfox.documentation.builders.PathSelectors;
import springfox.documentation.builders.RequestHandlerSelectors;
import springfox.documentation.service.ApiInfo;
import springfox.documentation.service.Contact;
import springfox.documentation.spi.DocumentationType;
import springfox.documentation.spring.web.plugins.Docket;
import java.util.Collections;

@Configuration
public class SwaggerConfiguration {

    @Bean
    public Docket apiV1() {
        return new Docket(DocumentationType.SWAGGER_2)
                .select()
                .apis(RequestHandlerSelectors.any())
```

```
                .paths(PathSelectors.regex("/v1/*.*"))
                .build()
                .apiInfo(apiInfo("v1"))
                .groupName("v1")
                .useDefaultResponseMessages(false);
    }

    @Bean
    public Docket apiV2() {
        return new Docket(DocumentationType.SWAGGER_2)
                .select()
                .apis(RequestHandlerSelectors.any())
                .paths(PathSelectors.regex("/v2/*.*"))
                .build()
                .apiInfo(apiInfo("v2"))
                .groupName("v2")
                .useDefaultResponseMessages(false);
    }

    private ApiInfo apiInfo(String version) {
        return new ApiInfo(
                "QuickPoll REST API",
                "QuickPoll Api for creating and managing polls",
                version,
                "Terms of service",
                new Contact("Maxim Bartkov", "www.linkedin.com/in/bartkov-
                maxim", "maxgalayoutop@gmail.com"),
                "MIT License", "http://opensource.org/licenses/MIT",
                Collections.emptyList());
    }

}
```

With this newly refactored SwaggerConfig, restart the QuickPoll application and launch Swagger UI in a web browser at http://localhost:8080/swagger-ui/index.html. After the UI has launched, append the request parameter ?group=v2 to the http://localhost:8080/v2/api-docs URI in the Swagger UI's input box and hit Explore. You should see and interact with the v2 version of the API as shown in Figure 7-1.

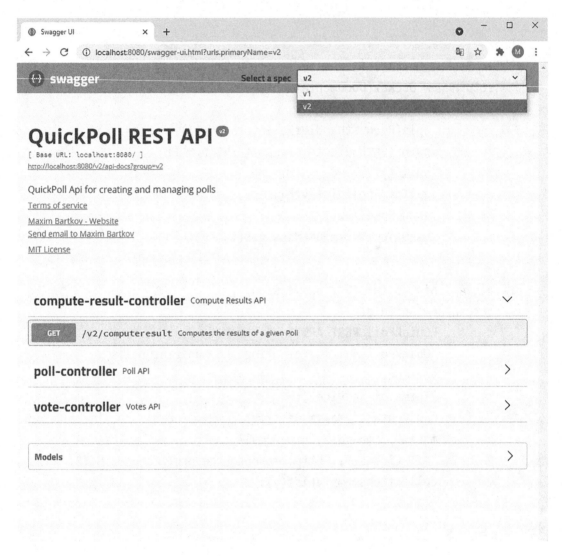

Figure 7-1. *Swagger UI for QuickPoll 2.0 version*

This concludes the configuration needed to version our QuickPoll application and sets the stage for adding pagination and sorting support in the final two sections of this chapter.

Pagination

REST APIs are consumed by a variety of clients ranging from desktop applications to Web to mobile devices. Hence, while designing a REST API capable of returning vast datasets, it is important to limit the amount of data returned for bandwidth and performance reasons. The bandwidth concerns become more important in the case of mobile clients consuming the API. Limiting the data can vastly improve the server's ability to retrieve data faster from a datastore and the client's ability to process the data and render the UI. By splitting the data into discrete pages or *paging data*, REST services allow clients to scroll through and access the entire dataset in manageable chunks.

Before we start implementing pagination in our QuickPoll application, let's look at four different pagination styles: page number pagination, limit offset pagination, cursor-based pagination, and time-based pagination.

Page Number Pagination

In this pagination style, the clients specify a page number containing the data they need. For example, a client wanting all the blog posts in page 3 of our hypothetical blog service can use the following GET method:

```
http://blog.example.com/posts?page=3
```

The REST service in this scenario would respond with a set of posts. The number of posts returned depends on the default page size set in the service. It is possible for the client to override the default page size by passing in a page-size parameter:

```
http://blog.example.com/posts?page=3&size=20
```

GitHub's REST services use this pagination style. By default, the page size is set to 30 but can be overridden using the per_page parameter:

```
https://api.github.com/user/repos?page=2&per_page=100
```

Limit Offset Pagination

In this pagination style, the client uses two parameters: a limit and an offset to retrieve the data that they need. The limit parameter indicates the maximum number of elements to return, and the offset parameter indicates the starting point for the return data. For example, to retrieve 10 blog posts starting from the item number 31, a client can use the following request:

```
http://blog.example.com/posts?limit=10&offset=30
```

Cursor-Based Pagination

In this pagination style, the clients make use of a *pointer or a cursor* to navigate through the dataset. A cursor is a service-generated random character string that acts as a marker for an item in the dataset. To understand this style, consider a client making the following request to get blog posts:

```
http://blog.example.com/posts
```

On receiving the request, the service would send data similar to this:

```
{
     "data" :      [
                   ... Blog data
                         ],
          "cursors" : {
                   "prev" : null,
                   "next" : "123asdf456iamcur"
                     }
}
```

This response contains a set of blogs representing a subset of the total dataset. The cursors that are part of the response contain a prev field that can be used to retrieve the previous subset of the data. However, because this is the initial subset, the prev field value is empty. The client can use the cursor value in the next field to get the next subset of the data using the following request:

```
http://api.example.com/posts?cursor=123asdf456iamcur
```

On receiving this request, the service would send the data along with the prev and next cursor fields. This pagination style is used by applications such as Twitter and Facebook that deal with real-time datasets (tweets and posts) where data changes frequently. The generated cursors typically don't live forever and should be used for short-term pagination purposes only.

Time-Based Pagination

In this style of pagination, the client specifies a timeframe to retrieve the data in which they are interested. Facebook supports this pagination style and requires time specified as a Unix timestamp. These are two Facebook example requests:

```
https://graph.facebook.com/me/feed?limit=25&until=1364587774
https://graph.facebook.com/me/feed?limit=25&since=1364849754
```

Both examples use the limit parameter to indicate the maximum number of items to be returned. The *until* parameter specifies the end of the time range, whereas the *since* parameter specifies the beginning of the time range.

Pagination Data

All the pagination styles in the previous sections return only a subset of the data. So, in addition to supplying the requested data, it becomes important for the service to communicate pagination-specific information such as total number of records or total number of pages or current page number and page size. The following example shows a response body with pagination information:

```
{
    "data": [
        ... Blog Data
    ],
    "totalPages": 9,
    "currentPageNumber": 2,
    "pageSize": 10,
    "totalRecords": 90
}
```

Clients can use the pagination information to assess the current state as well as construct URLs to obtain the next or previous datasets. The other technique services employ is to include the pagination information in a special Link header. The Link header is defined as part of RFC 5988 (http://tools.ietf.org/html/rfc5988). It typically contains a set of ready-made links to scroll forward and backward. GitHub uses this approach; here is an example of a Link header value:

```
Link: <https://api.github.com/user/repos?page=3&per_page=100>; rel="next",
<https://api.github.com/user/repos?page=50&per_page=100>; rel="last"
```

QuickPoll Pagination

To support large poll datasets in a QuickPoll application, we will be implementing the page number pagination style and will include the paging information in the response body.

We begin the implementation by configuring our QuickPoll application to load dummy poll data into its database during the bootstrapping process. This would enable us to test our polling and sorting code. To achieve this, copy the import.sql file from the downloaded chapter code into src\main\resources folder. The import.sql file contains DML statements for creating test polls. Hibernate out of the box loads the import.sql file found under the classpath and executes all of the SQL statements in it. Restart the QuickPoll application, and navigate to http://localhost:8080/v2/polls in Postman; it should list all of the loaded test polls.

Spring Data JPA and Spring MVC provides out-of-the-box support for the page number pagination style, making our QuickPoll paging implementation easy. Central to paging (and sorting) functionality in Spring Data JPA is the org.springframework.data. repository.PagingAndSortingRepository interface shown in Listing 7-4.

Listing 7-4. Spring Data JPA's Paging and Sorting Repository

```
public interface PagingAndSortingRepository<T, ID extends Serializable>
extends CrudRepository<T, ID> {
    Page<T> findAll(Pageable pageable);
    Iterable<T> findAll(Sort sort);
}
```

The `PagingAndSortingRepository` interface extends the `CrudRepository` interface that we have been using so far in the QuickPoll application. Additionally, it adds two finder methods that return entities matching the paging and sorting criteria provided. The `findAll` method responsible for paging takes a `Pageable` instance to read information such as page size and page number. Additionally, it also takes sorting information, which we will zoom in on in a later section of this chapter. This `findAll` method returns a `Page` instance that contains the data subset and the following information:

- Total elements—Total elements in the result set

- Number of elements—Number of elements in the returned subset

- Size—The maximum number of elements in each page

- Total pages—Total number of pages in the result set

- Number—Returns the current page number

- Last—Flag indicating if it is the last data subset

- First—Flag indicating if it is the first data subset

- Sort—Returns parameters used for sorting, if any

The next step in implementing paging in QuickPoll is to make our `PollRepository` extend `PagingAndSortingRepository` instead of current `CrudRepository`. Listing 7-5 shows the new `PollRepository` implementation. Because the `PagingAndSortingRepository` extends the `CrudRepository`, all of the functionality needed for the first version of our API remains intact.

Listing 7-5. PollRepository Implementation

```
package com.apress.repository;

import org.springframework.data.repository.PagingAndSortingRepository;
import com.apress.domain.Poll;
public interface PollRepository extends PagingAndSortingRepository<Poll,
Long> {

}
```

Changing the repository to use `PagingAndSortingRepository` concludes our backend implementation needed for paging. We now move on to refactoring the V2 `PollController` so that it uses the new paging finder method. Listing 7-6 shows the refactored `getAllPolls` method of the V2 `com.apress.v2.controller.PollController`. Notice that we have added the `Pageable` parameter to the `getAllPolls` method. On receiving a GET request on `"/polls,"` Spring MVC inspects the request parameters, constructs a `Pageable` instance, and passes it to the `getAllPolls` method. Typically, the passed-in instance is of the type `PageRequest`. The `Pageable` parameter is then passed to the new finder method, and the paged data is retuned as part of the response.

Listing 7-6. GetAllPolls Method with Paging Functionality

```
import org.springframework.data.domain.Page;
import org.springframework.data.domain.Pageable;

@RequestMapping(value="/polls", method=RequestMethod.GET)
@ApiOperation(value = "Retrieves all the polls", response=Poll.class,
responseContainer="List")
public ResponseEntity<Page<Poll>> getAllPolls(Pageable pageable) {
        Page<Poll> allPolls = pollRepository.findAll(pageable);
        return new ResponseEntity<>(allPolls, HttpStatus.OK);
}
```

This concludes the QuickPoll pagination implementation. Restart the QuickPoll application, and submit a GET request to `http://localhost:8080/v2/polls?page=0&size=2` using Postman. The response should contain two poll instances with paging-related metadata. Figure 7-2 shows the request as well as the metadata portion of the response.

Get All Polls V2 Paging

Figure 7-2. *Paged results along with paging metadata*

Note   Spring Data JPA uses a zero index–based paging approach. Hence, the first page number starts with 0 and not 1.

Changing Default Page Size

Spring MVC uses an `org.springframework.data.web.PageableHandler`
`MethodArgumentResolver` to extract paging information from the request parameters and inject `Pageable` instances into Controller methods. Out of the box, the `PageableHandlerMethodArgumentResolver` class sets the default page size to 20. Hence, if you perform a GET request on `http://localhost:8080/v2/polls`, the response would include 20 polls. Although 20 is a good default page size, there might be occasions when you might want to change it globally in your application. To do this, you need to create and register a new instance of `PageableHandlerMethodArgumentResolver` with the settings of your choice.

Spring Boot applications requiring changes to default MVC behavior need to create classes of type `org.springframework.web.servlet.config.annotation.WebMvcConfigurer` and use its callback methods for customization. Listing 7-7 shows the newly created `QuickPollMvcConfigAdapter` class in the `com.apress` package with the configuration to set the default page size to 5. Here we are using the `WebMvcConfigurer`'s `addArgumentResolvers` callback method. We begin the method implementation by creating an instance of `PageableHandlerMethodArgumentResolver`. The `setFallbackPageable` method, as the name suggests, is used by Spring MVC when no paging information is found in the request parameters. We create a `PageRequest` instance with 5 as the default page size and pass it to the `setFallbackPageable` method. We then register our `PageableHandlerMethodArgumentResolver` instance with Spring using the passed-in `argumentResolvers` parameter.

Listing 7-7. Code to Change Default Page Size to 5

```
package com.apress;

import java.util.List;
import org.springframework.context.annotation.Configuration;
import org.springframework.data.domain.PageRequest;
import org.springframework.data.web.PageableHandlerMethodArgumentResolver;
import org.springframework.web.method.support.
HandlerMethodArgumentResolver;
import org.springframework.web.servlet.config.annotation.WebMvcConfigurer;

@Configuration
public class QuickPollMvcConfigAdapter implements WebMvcConfigurer {

        @Override

public void addArgumentResolvers(List<HandlerMethodArgumentResolver>
argumentResolvers) {

PageableHandlerMethodArgumentResolver phmar = new
PageableHandlerMethodArgumentResolver();
            // Set the default size to 5
            phmar.setFallbackPageable(PageRequest.of(0, 5));
            argumentResolvers.add(phmar);
        }
}
```

Restart the QuickPoll application and perform a GET request on `http://localhost:8080/v2/polls` using Postman. You will notice that the response now includes only five polls. The associated paging metadata is shown in Listing 7-8.

Listing 7-8. Paging Metadata for Default Page Size 5

```
{
    ..... Omitted Poll Data ......

    "totalPages": 4,
    "totalElements": 20,
    "last": false,
    "size": 5,
    "number": 0,
    "sort": null,
    "numberOfElements": 5,
    "first": true
}
```

Sorting

Sorting allows REST clients to determine the order in which items in a dataset are arranged. REST services supporting sorting allow clients to submit parameters with properties to be used for sorting. For example, a client can submit the following request to sort blog posts based on their created date and title:

`http://blog.example.com/posts?sort=createdDate,title`

Sort Ascending or Sort Descending

The REST services can also allow the clients to specify one of the two sort directions: ascending or descending. Because there is no set standard around this, the following examples showcase popular ways for specifying sort direction:

`http://blog.example.com/posts?sortByDesc=createdDate&sortByAsc=title`
`http://blog.example.com/posts?sort=createdDate,desc&sort=title,asc`
`http://blog.example.com/posts?sort=-createdDate,title`

In all of these examples, we are retrieving blog posts in the descending order of their created date. Posts with the same created date are then sorted based on their titles:

- In the first approach, the sort parameter clearly specifies if the direction should be ascending or descending.

- In the second approach, we have used the same parameter name for both directions. However, the parameter value spells out the sort direction.

- The last approach uses the "-" notation to indicate that any property prefixed with a "-" should be sorted on a descending direction. Properties that are not prefixed with a "-" will be sorted in the ascending direction.

QuickPoll Sorting

Considering that sorting is typically used in conjunction with paging, Spring Data JPA's PagingAndSortingRepository and Pageable implementations are designed to handle and service sorting requests from the ground up. Hence, we don't require any explicit implementation for sorting.

To test sorting functionality, submit a GET request to http://localhost:8080/v2/polls/?sort=question using Postman. You should see the response with Polls sorted in ascending order of their question text along with sort metadata. Figure 7-3 shows the Postman request along with the sort metadata.

Get All Polls V2 Sorting

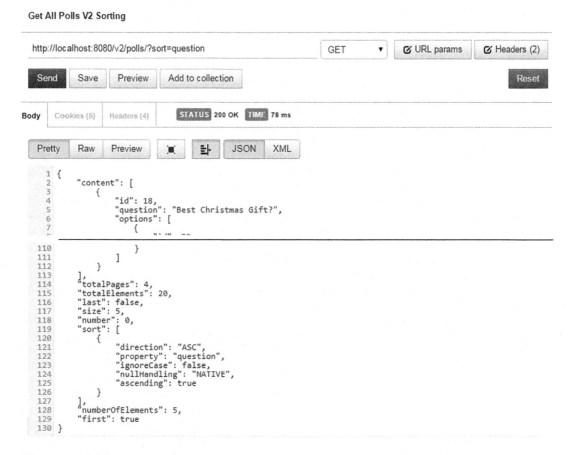

Figure 7-3. *Sort metadata*

To sort on multiple fields with different sort directions, Spring MVC requires you to follow the second approach discussed in the previous section. The following request sorts on ascending question value and descending id value:

```
http://localhost:8080/v2/polls/?sort=question,asc&sort=id,desc
```

Summary

In this chapter we reviewed the different strategies for versioning REST API. We then implemented versioning in QuickPoll using the URL versioning approach. We also reviewed the different approaches for dealing with large datasets using pagination and sorting techniques. Finally, we used Spring Data's out-of-the-box functionality to implement page number pagination style. In the next chapter, we will review strategies for securing REST services.

167

CHAPTER 8

Security

In this chapter we will discuss the following:

- Strategies for securing REST services
- OAuth 2.0
- Basics of the Spring Security framework
- Implementing QuickPoll security

Traditional web applications requiring security typically use username/passwords for identification purposes. REST services pose interesting security problems as they can be consumed by a variety of clients such as browsers and mobile devices. They can also be consumed by other services, and this machine-to-machine communication might not have any human interaction. It is also not uncommon for clients to consume REST services on behalf of a user. In this chapter, we will explore the different authentication/ authorization approaches that can be used while working with REST services. Then we will look at using some of these approaches to secure our QuickPoll application.

Securing REST Services

We begin with a survey of six popular approaches that are used for securing REST services:

- Session-based security
- HTTP Basic authentication
- Digest authentication
- Certificate-based security
- XAuth
- OAuth

169

© Balaji Varanasi and Maxim Bartkov 2022
B. Varanasi and M. Bartkov, *Spring REST*, https://doi.org/10.1007/978-1-4842-7477-4_8

Session-Based Security

The session-based security model relies on a server side session to hold on to a user's identity across requests. In a typical web application, when a user tries to access a protected resource, they are presented with a login page. On successful authentication, the server stores the logged-in user's information in an HTTP session. On subsequent requests, the session is queried to retrieve the user's information and is used to perform authorization checks. If the user doesn't have the proper authorization, their request will be denied. Figure 8-1 is a pictorial representation of this approach.

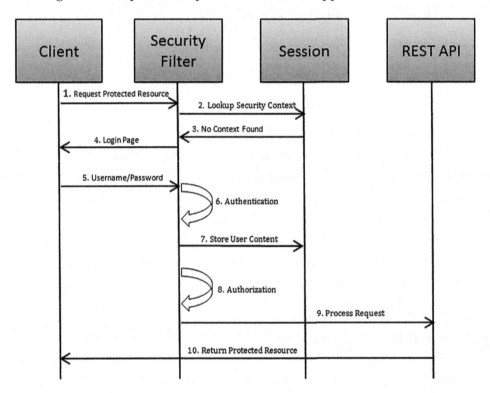

Figure 8-1. *Session-based security flow*

Frameworks such as Spring Security provide all the necessary plumbing to develop applications using this security model. This approach is very appealing to developers that are adding REST services to existing Spring Web applications. The REST services will retrieve the user identity from the session to perform authorization checks and serve resources accordingly. However, this approach violates the statelessness REST constraint. Also, because the server holds the client's state, this approach is not scalable. Ideally, the client should hold the state and server should be stateless.

HTTP Basic Authentication

Using a login form to capture a username and password is possible when there is human interaction involved. However, this might not be possible when we have services talking to other services. HTTP Basic authentication provides a mechanism that allows clients to send authentication information using both interactive and noninteractive fashions.

In this approach, when a client makes a request to a protected resource, the server sends a 401 "Unauthorized" response code and a "WWW-Authenticate" header. The "Basic" portion of the header indicates that we will be using Basic authentication and the "realm" portion indicates a protected space on the server:

```
GET /protected_resource
401 Unauthorized
WWW-Authenticate: Basic realm="Example Realm"
```

On receiving the response, the client concatenates a username and password with a semicolon and Base64 encodes the concatenated string. It then sends that information over to the server using a standard Authorization header:

```
GET /protected_resource
Authorization: Basic bHxpY26U5lkjfdk
```

The server decodes the submitted information and validates the submitted credentials. On successful verification, the server completes the request. The entire flow is shown in Figure 8-2.

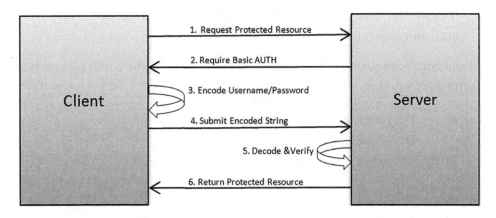

Figure 8-2. *HTTP Basic authentication flow*

Because the client includes the authentication information in each request, the server becomes stateless. It is important to remember that the client is simply encoding the information and not encrypting it. Hence, on non-SSL/TLS connections, it is possible to conduct a man-in-the-middle attack and steal the password.

Digest Authentication

The Digest authentication approach is similar to the Basic authentication model discussed earlier except that the user credentials are sent encrypted. The client submits a request for a protected resource and the server responds with a 401 "Unauthorized" response code and a WWW-Authenticate header. Here is an example of a server response:

```
GET /protected_resource
401 Unauthorized
WWW-Authenticate: Digest realm="Example Realm", nonce="P35kl89sdfghERT10
Asdfnbvc", qop="auth"
```

Notice that the WWW-Authenticate specifies the Digest authentication scheme along with a server-generated nonce and a qop. A nonce is an arbitrary token used for cryptographic purposes. The qop, or "quality of protection," directive can contain two values—"auth" or "auth-int":

- A qop value "auth" indicates that the digest is used for authentication purposes.

- A value "auth-int" indicates that digest will be used for authentication and request integrity.

On receiving the request, if the qop value is set to "auth," the client generates a digest using this formula:

```
hash_value_1 = MD5(username:realm:password)
has_value_2 = MD5(request_method:request_uri) .
digest = MD5(hash_value_1:nonce:hash_value_2)
```

If the qop value is set to `"auth-int,"` the client computes the digest by including the request body:

```
hash_value_1 = MD5(username:realm:password)
has_value_2 = MD5(request_method:request_uri:MD5(request_body))
digest = MD5(hash_value_1:nonce:hash_value_2)
```

By default, the MD5 algorithm is used to compute the hash values. The digest is included in the `Authorization` header and is sent to the server. On receiving the request, the server computes the digest and verifies the user's identity. On successful verification, the server completes the request. A complete flow of this method is shown in Figure 8-3.

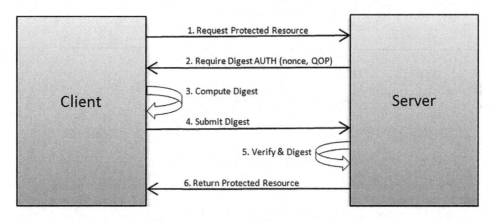

Figure 8-3. *Digest authentication flow*

The Digest authentication approach is more secure than the Basic authentication, as the password is never sent in clear text. However, on non-SSL/TLS communications, it is still possible for snoopers to retrieve the digest and replay the request. One way to address this problem is to limit server-generated nonces to one-time use only. Also, because the server has to generate the digest for verification, it needs to have access to the plain text version of the password. Hence, it can't employ more secure one-way encryption algorithms such as bcrypt and can become more vulnerable to server side attacks.

Certificate-Based Security

The certificate-based security model relies on certificates to verify a party's identity. In an SSL/TLS-based communication, a client such as a browser often verifies the server's identity using certificates to ensure that the server is what it claims to be. This model can be extended to perform mutual authentication where a server can request a client certificate as part of an SSL/TLS handshake and verify a client's identity.

In this approach, on receiving a request for a protected resource, the server presents its certificate to the client. The client ensures that a trusted Certificate Authority (CA) issued the server's certificate and sends its certificate over to the server. The server verifies the client's certificate and, on successful verification, will grant access to the protected resource. This flow is shown in Figure 8-4.

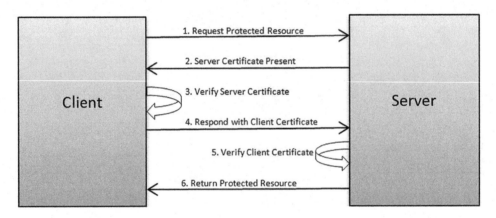

Figure 8-4. *Certificate-based security flow*

The certificate-based security model eliminates the need to send over a shared secret, making it more secure over username/password models. However, deployments and maintenance of certificates can be expensive and typically are used for large systems.

XAuth

As REST APIs became popular, the number of third-party applications that use those APIs also grew significantly. These applications need a username and password in order to interact with REST services and perform actions on behalf of users. This poses a huge security problem as third-party applications now have access to usernames and passwords. A security breach in the third-party application can compromise user information. Also, if the user changes his credentials, he needs to remember to go and update all of these third-party applications. Finally, this mechanism doesn't allow the user to revoke his authorization to the third-party application. The only option for revoking in this case would be to change his password.

The XAuth and OAuth schemes provide a mechanism to access protected resources on a user's behalf without needing to store passwords. In this approach, a client application would request a username and password from the user typically by using a login form. The client would then send the username and password to the server. The server receives the user's credentials and validates them. On successful validation, a token is returned to the client. The client discards the username and password information and stores the token locally. When accessing a user's protected resource, the client would include the token in the request. This is typically accomplished using a custom HTTP header such as X-Auth-Token. The longevity of the token is dependent on the implementing service. The token can remain until the server revokes it or the token can expire in a designated period of time. This flow is shown in Figure 8-5.

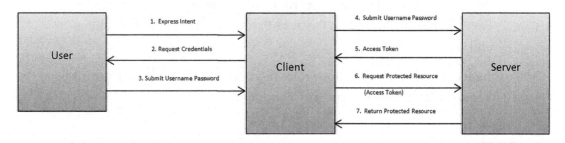

Figure 8-5. *XAuth security flow*

Applications such as Twitter allow third-party applications to access their REST API using an XAuth scheme. However, even with XAuth, a third-party application needs to capture a username and password, leaving the possibility of misuse. Considering the simplicity involved in XAuth, it might be a good candidate when the same organization develops the client as well as the REST API.

OAuth 2.0

The Open Authorization or OAuth is a framework for accessing protected resources on behalf of a user without storing a password. The OAuth protocol was first introduced in 2007 and was superseded by OAuth 2.0, which was introduced in 2010. In this book, we will be reviewing OAuth 2.0 and general principles.

OAuth 2.0 defines the following four roles:

- Resource owner—A resource owner is the user that wants to give access to portions of their account or resources. For example, a resource owner could be a Twitter or a Facebook user.

- Client—A client is an application that wants access to a user's resources. This could be a third-party app such as Klout (`https://klout.com/`) that wants to access a user's Twitter account.

- Authorization server—An authorization server verifies the user's identity and grants the client a token to access the user's resources.

- Resource server—A resource server hosts protected user resources. For example, this would be Twitter API to access tweets and timelines and so on.

The interactions between these four roles discussed are depicted in Figure 8-6. OAuth 2.0 requires these interactions to be conducted on SSL.

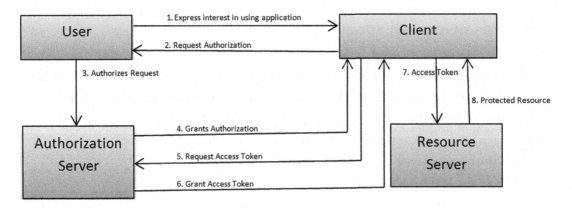

Figure 8-6. *OAuth 2.0 security flow*

Before a client can participate in the "OAuth dance" shown in Figure 8-6, it must register itself with the authorization server. For most public APIs such as Facebook and Twitter, this involves filling out an application form and providing information about the client such as application name, base domain, and website. On successful registration, the client will receive a Client ID and a Client secret. The Client ID is used to uniquely identify the Client and is available publicly. These client credentials play an important part in the OAuth interactions, which we will discuss in just a minute.

The OAuth interaction begins with the user expressing interest in using the "Client," a third-party application. The client requests authorization to access protected resources on the user's behalf and redirects the user/resource owner to the authorization server. An example URI that the client can redirect the user to is shown here:

```
https://oauth2.example.com/authorize?client_id=CLIENT_ID&response_
type=auth_code&call_back=CALL_BACK_URI&scope=read,tweet
```

The usage of HTTPS is mandatory for any production OAuth 2.0 interactions, and, hence, the URI begins with https. The CLIENT_ID is used to provide the client's identity to the authorization server. The scope parameter provides a comma-separated set of scopes/roles that the client needs.

On receiving the request, the authorization server would present the user with an authentication challenge typically via a login form. The user provides his username and password. On successful verification of the user credentials, the authorization server redirects the user to the client application using the CALL_BACK_URI parameter. The authorization server also appends an authorization code to the CALL_BACK_URI parameter value. Here is an example URL that an authorization server might generate:

```
https://mycoolclient.com/code_callback?auth_code=6F99A74F2D066A267D6D838F88
```

The client then uses the authorization code to request an access token from the authorization server. To achieve this, a client would typically perform an HTTP POST on a URI like this:

```
https://oauth2.example.com/access_token?client_id=CLIENT_ID&client_
secret=CLIENT_SECRET&
auth_code=6F99A74F2D066A267D6D838F88
```

As you can see, the client provides its credentials as part of the request. The authorization server verifies the client's identity and authorization code. On successful verification, it returns an access token. Here is an example response in JSON format:

```
{"access_token"="f292c6912e7710c8"}
```

On receiving the access token, the client will request a protected resource from the resource server passing in the access token it obtained. The resource server validates the access token and serves the protected resource.

OAuth Client Profiles

One of the strengths of OAuth 2.0 is its support for a variety of client profiles such as "web application," "native application," and "user agent/browser application." The authorization code flow discussed earlier (often referred to as *authorization grant type*) is applicable to "web application" clients that have a web-based user interface and a server side backend. This allows the client to store the authorization code in a secure backend and reuse it for future interactions. Other client profiles have their own flows that determine the interaction between the four OAuth 2.0 players.

A pure JavaScript-based application or a native application can't store authorization codes securely. Hence, for such clients, the callback from the authorization server doesn't include an authorization code. Instead, an *implicit grant-type* approach is taken and an access token is directly handed over to the client, which is then used for requesting protected resources. Applications falling under this client profile will not have a client secret and are simply identified using the client ID.

OAuth 2.0 also supports an authorization flow, referred to as *password grant type* that is similar to XAuth discussed in the previous section. In this flow, the user supplies his credentials to the client application directly. He is never redirected to the authorization server. The client passes these credentials to the authorization server and receives an access token for requesting protected resources.

OAuth 1.0 introduced several implementation complexities especially around the cryptographic requirements for signing requests with client credentials. OAuth 2.0 simplified this by eliminating signatures and requiring HTTPS for all interactions. However, because many of OAuth 2's features are optional, the specification has resulted in non-interoperable implementations.

Refresh Tokens versus Access Tokens

The lifetime of access tokens can be limited and clients should be prepared for the possibility of a token no longer working. To prevent the need for the resource owner to repeatedly authenticate, the OAuth 2.0 specification has provided a notion of refresh tokens. An authorization server can optionally issue a refresh token when it generates an access token. The client stores this refresh token, and when an access token expires, it contacts the authorization server for a fresh set of access token as well as refresh token. Specification allows generation of refresh tokens for authorization and password grant-type flows. Considering the lack of security with the "implicit grant type," refresh tokens are prohibited for such client profiles.

Spring Security Overview

To implement security in the QuickPoll application, we will be using another popular Spring subproject, namely, Spring Security. Before we move forward with the implementation, let's understand Spring Security and the different components that make up the framework.

Spring Security, formerly known as Acegi Security, is a framework for securing Java-based applications. It provides an out-of-the-box integration to a variety of authentication systems such as LDAP, Kerberos, OpenID, OAuth, and so on. With minimal configuration, it can be easily extended to work with any custom authentication and authorization systems. The framework also implements security best practices and has inbuilt features to protect against attacks such as CSRF, or Cross-Site Request Forgery, session fixation, and so on.

Spring Security provides a consistent security model that can be used to secure web URLs and Java methods. The high-level steps involved during the Spring Security authentication/authorization process along with components involved are listed here:

1. The process begins with a user requesting a protected resource on a Spring-secured web application.

2. The request goes through a series of Spring Security filters referred to as a "filter chain" that identify an `org.springframework.security.web.AuthenticationEntryPoint` to service the request.

The AuthenticationEntryPoint will respond to the client with a request to authentication. This is done, for example, by sending a login page to the user.

3. On receiving authentication information from the user such as a username/password, a org.springframework.security.core. Authentication object is created. The Authentication interface is shown in Listing 8-1, and its implementation plays a dual role in Spring Security. They represent a token for an authentication request or a fully authenticated principal after authentication is successfully completed. The isAuthenticated method can be used to determine the current role played by an Authentication instance. In case of a username/password authentication, the getPrincipal method returns the username and the getCredentials returns the password. The getUserDetails method contains additional information such as IP address and so on.

Listing 8-1. Authentication API

```
public interface Authentication extends Principal, Serializable {

        Object getPrincipal();
        Object getCredentials();
        Object getDetails();
        Collection<? extends GrantedAuthority> getAuthorities();
        boolean isAuthenticated();

void setAuthenticated(boolean isAuthenticated) throws
IllegalArgumentException;
}
```

4. As a next step, the authentication request token is presented to an org.springframework.security.authentication. AuthenticationManager. The AuthenticationManager, as shown in Listing 8-2, contains an authenticate method that takes an authentication request token and returns a fully

populated Authentication instance. Spring provides an out-of-the-box implementation of AuthenticationManager called ProviderManager.

Listing 8-2. AuthenticationManager API

```
public interface AuthenticationManager {

Authentication authenticate(Authentication authentication)
throws AuthenticationException;

}
```

5. In order to perform authentication, the ProviderManager needs to compare the submitted user information with a backend user store such as LDAP or database. ProviderManager delegates this responsibility to a series of org.springframework. security.authentication.AuthenticationProvider. These AuthenticationProviders use an org.springframework. security.core.userdetails.UserDetailsService to retrieve user information from backend stores. Listing 8-3 shows the UserDetailsService API.

Listing 8-3. UserDetailsService API

```
public interface UserDetailsService {

UserDetails loadUserByUsername(String username)
throws UsernameNotFoundException;
}
```

Implementations of UserDetailsService such as JdbcDaoImpl and LdapUserDetailService will use the passed-in username to retrieve user information. These implementations will also create a set of GrantedAuthority instances that represent roles/ authorities the user has in the system.

6. The `AuthenticationProvider` compares the submitted credentials with the information in the backend system, and on successful verification, the `org.springframework.security.core.userdetails.UserDetails` object is used to build a fully populated `Authentication` instance.

7. The `Authentication` instance is then put into an `org.springframework.security.core.context.SecurityContextHolder`. The `SecurityContextHolder,` as the name suggests, simply associates the logged-in user's context with the current thread of execution so that it is readily available across user requests or operations. In a web-based application, the logged-in user's context is typically stored in the user's HTTP session.

8. Spring Security then performs an authorization check using an `org.springframework.security.access.intercept.AbstractSecurityInterceptor` and its implementations `org.springframework.security.web.access.intercept.FilterSecurityInterceptor` and `org.springframework.security.access.intercept.aopalliance.MethodSecurityInterceptor`. The `FilterSecurityInterceptor` is used for URL-based authorization and `MethodSecurityInterceptor` is used for method invocation authorization.

9. The `AbstractSecurityInterceptor` relies on security configuration and a set of `org.springframework.security.access.AccessDecisionManagers` to decide if the user is authorized or not. On successful authorization, the user is given access to the protected resource.

Note   To keep things simple, I have purposefully omitted some Spring Security classes in these steps. For a complete review of Spring Security and the authentication/authorization steps, please refer to *Pro Spring Security* (Apress, 2019).

Now that you have a basic understanding of Spring Security's authentication/
authorization flow as well as some of its components, let's look at integrating Spring
Security into our QuickPoll application.

Securing QuickPoll

We will implement security in the QuickPoll application to meet the following two
requirements:

- Registered users can create and access polls. This allows us to keep
  track of accounts, usage, and so on.

- Polls can be deleted only by users with admin privileges

Note   In this chapter, we will continue building on the work that we did on the
QuickPoll application in the previous chapters. Alternatively, a starter project is
available for you to use inside the `Chapter8\starter` folder of the downloaded
source code. In this chapter, we will secure QuickPoll using Basic authentication.
Then we will add OAuth 2.0 support to QuickPoll. Hence, the `Chapter8\final`
folder contains two folders: `quick-poll-ch8-final-basic-auth` and `quick-poll-ch8-final`. The `quick-poll-ch8-final-basic-auth` contains
the solution with Basic authentication added to QuickPoll. The `quick-poll-ch8-final` contains the completed solution with both Basic authentication and
OAuth 2.0 added. We understand that not all projects need OAuth 2.0 support.
Hence, splitting the final solution into two projects allows you to examine and
use features/code that you need. Please refer to the solutions under the `final`
folder for complete listings containing getters/setters and additional imports.
The downloaded `Chapter8` folder also contains an exported Postman collection
containing REST API requests associated with this chapter.

By requiring user authentication, we will be drastically changing the behavior of
the QuickPoll application. To allow existing users to continue using our QuickPoll
application, we will create a new version (v3) of our API to implement these changes.
To accomplish this, create a new `com.apress.v3.controller` package under `src\main\
java` and copy controllers from the `com.apress.v2.controller` package. For the newly

copied controllers, change the RequestMappings from "/v2/" to "/v3/" and change the controller name prefixes from v2 to v3 to reflect version 3 of the API. We start the implementation by adding the Spring Security starter dependency shown in Listing 8-4 to QuickPoll project's pom.xml file. This would bring in all Spring Security–related JAR files into the project.

Listing 8-4. Spring Starter POM

```
<dependency>
        <groupId>org.springframework.boot</groupId>
        <artifactId>spring-boot-starter-security</artifactId>
</dependency>
```

On seeing Spring Security in the classpath, Spring Boot adds default security configuration that secures all of the HTTP endpoints with an HTTP basic authentication. Start the QuickPoll application, and submit a GET request to http://localhost:8080/v3/polls using Postman. Postman displays an authentication window prompting you to enter a username and password, as shown in Figure 8-7.

Figure 8-7. *Basic authentication window in Postman*

Spring Boot's default security configuration comes with a single user with username user. Spring Boot generates a random password for the user and prints it at INFO log level during application startup. In your console/log file, you should see an entry like this one:

```
Using default security password: 554cc6c2-67e1-4f1e-8c5b-096609e2d0b1
```

Enter the username and password found in your console into the Postmaster login window and hit Log In. Spring Security will validate the entered credentials and allow the request to be completed.

cURL

Up to this point, we have been using Postman for testing our QuickPoll application. In this chapter, we will be using a command line tool named cURL in conjunction with Postman. cURL is a popular open-source tool used for interacting with servers and transferring data with URL syntax. It comes installed in most operating system distributions. If cURL is not available on your system, follow the instructions at `http://curl.haxx.se/download.html` to download and install cURL on your machine. Refer to Appendix A for instructions on installing cURL on a Windows machine.

To test our QuickPoll Basic authentication using cURL, run the following command at command line:

```
curl -vu user:554cc6c2-67e1-4f1e-8c5b-096609e2d0b1 http://localhost:8080/
v3/polls
```

In this command, the -v option requests cURL to run in the debug mode (verbose). The -u option allows us to specify the username and password needed for Basic authentication. A full list of cURL options is available at `http://curl.haxx.se/docs/manual.html`.

User Infrastructure Setup

Although Spring Boot has simplified Spring Security integration significantly, we would like to customize security behavior so that it uses application users instead of Spring Boot's generic user. We also would like to apply the security to the v3 `PollController`, leaving other endpoints to be accessed anonymously. Before we look at customizing Spring Security, let's set up the infrastructure needed for creating/updating QuickPoll application users.

We start by creating a `User` domain object as shown in Listing 8-5 to represent a QuickPoll user. The `User` class contains attributes such as `username`, `password`, `firstname`, and `lastname`. It also contains a Boolean flag to indicate if the user has administrative privileges. As a security best practice, we have annotated the `password` field with @JsonIgnore. Therefore, the password field will not be included in a user's representation, thereby preventing clients from accessing the password value. Because "User" is a keyword in databases such as Oracle, we have used the @Table annotation to give the name "Users" to table corresponding to this User entity.

Listing 8-5. User Class

```
package com.apress.domain;

import javax.persistence.Table;
import org.hibernate.annotations.Type;
import com.fasterxml.jackson.annotation.JsonIgnore;
import org.hibernate.annotations.Type;
import javax.validation.constraints.NotEmpty;

@Entity
@Table(name="USERS")
public class User {

        @Id
        @GeneratedValue
        @Column(name="USER_ID")
        private Long id;

        @Column(name="USERNAME")
        @NotEmpty
        private String username;

        @Column(name="PASSWORD")
        @NotEmpty
        @JsonIgnore
        private String password;

        @Column(name="FIRST_NAME")
        @NotEmpty
        private String firstName;

        @Column(name="LAST_NAME")
        @NotEmpty
        private String lastName;
```

```
@Column(name="ADMIN", columnDefinition="char(3)")
@Type(type="yes_no")
@NotEmpty
private boolean admin;

    // Getters and Setters omitted for brevity
}
```

We will be storing the QuickPoll users in a database and hence will require a UserRepository to perform CRUD actions on the User entity. Listing 8-6 shows the UserRepository interface created under com.apress.repository package. In addition to the finder methods provided by the CrudRepository, the UserRepository contains a custom finder method named findByUsername. Spring Data JPA would provide a runtime implementation so that the findByUsername method retrieves a user associated with the passed-in username parameter.

Listing 8-6. UserRepository Interface

```
package com.apress.repository;

import org.springframework.data.repository.CrudRepository;
import com.apress.domain.User;

public interface UserRepository extends CrudRepository<User, Long> {
        public User findByUsername(String username);
}
```

Applications such as QuickPoll typically have an interface that allows new users to register. To keep things simple for the purposes of this book, we have generated some test users shown in Listing 8-7. Copy these SQL statements to the end of import.sql file under the QuickPoll project's src\main\resources folder. When the application gets bootstrapped, Hibernate will load these test users into the "Users" table and make them available for the application's use.

Listing 8-7. Test User Data

```
insert into users (user_id, username, password, first_name, last_name,
admin) values
(1, 'mickey', '$2a$10$kSqU.ek5pDRMMK21tHJlceS1xOc9Kna4FODD2ZwQH/
LAzHOMLOp6.', 'Mickey', 'Mouse', 'no');
insert into users (user_id, username, password, first_name, last_name,
admin) values
(2, 'minnie', '$2a$10$MnHcLn.XdLx.iMntXsmdgeO1B4wAW1E5GOy/
VrLUmr4aAzabXnGFq', 'Minnie', 'Mouse', 'no');
insert into users (user_id, username, password, first_name, last_name,
admin) values
(3, 'donald', '$2a$10$OUCBIO4PCXiKOpF/9kI7.uAXiHNQeeHdkv9NhA1/
xgmRpfd4qxRMG', 'Donald', 'Duck', 'no');
insert into users (user_id, username, password, first_name, last_name,
admin) values
(4, 'daisy', '$2a$10$aNoR88g5b5TzSKb7mQ1nQOkyEwfHVQOxHYOHX7irI8qWINvLDWR
yS', 'Daisy', 'Duck', 'no');
insert into users (user_id, username, password, first_name, last_name,
admin) values
(5, 'clarabelle', '$2a$10$cuTJd2ayEwXfsPdoF5/hde6gzsPx/
gEiv8LZsjPN9VPoN5XVR8cKW', 'Clarabelle', 'Cow', 'no');
insert into users (user_id, username, password, first_name, last_name,
admin) values
(6, 'admin', '$2a$10$JQOfG5Tqnf97SbGcKsalz.
XpDQbXi1APOf2SHPVW27bWNioi9nI8y', 'Super', 'Admin', 'yes');
```

Notice that the password for the generated test users is not in plain text. Following good security practices, I have encrypted the password values using the BCrypt (http://en.wikipedia.org/wiki/Bcrypt) adaptive hashing function. Table 8-1 shows these test users and their plain text version of passwords.

Table 8-1. *Test User Information*

Username	Password	Is admin
Mickey	Cheese	No
Minnie	Red01	No
Donald	Quack	No
Daisy	Quack2	No
Clarabelle	Moo	No
Admin	Admin	Yes

UserDetailsService Implementation

In the Spring Security introduction section, we learned that a UserDetailsService is typically used to retrieve user information, which gets compared with user-submitted credentials during the authentication process. Listing 8-8 shows a UserDetailsService implementation for our QuickPoll application.

Listing 8-8. UserDetailsService Implementation for QuickPoll

```
package com.apress.security;

import javax.inject.Inject;
import org.springframework.security.core.GrantedAuthority;
import org.springframework.security.core.authority.AuthorityUtils;
import org.springframework.security.core.userdetails.UserDetails;
import org.springframework.security.core.userdetails.UserDetailsService;
import org.springframework.security.core.userdetails.
UsernameNotFoundException;
import org.springframework.stereotype.Component;
import com.apress.domain.User;
import com.apress.repository.UserRepository;
```

```
@Component
public class QuickPollUserDetailsService implements UserDetailsService {

        @Inject
        private UserRepository userRepository;

        @Override

public UserDetails loadUserByUsername(String username) throws
UsernameNotFoundException {

                User user = userRepository.findByUsername(username);

                if(user == null) {

throw new UsernameNotFoundException(String.format("User with the username
%s doesn't exist", username));
                }

                // Create a granted authority based on user's role.

// Can't pass null authorities to user. Hence initialize with an
empty arraylist
                List<GrantedAuthority> authorities = new ArrayList<>();
                if(user.isAdmin()) {
                        authorities = AuthorityUtils.createAuthorityList
                        ("ROLE_ADMIN");
                }

                // Create a UserDetails object from the data

UserDetails userDetails = new org.springframework.security.core.
userdetails.User(user.getUsername(), user.getPassword(), authorities);

                return userDetails;
        }
}
```

The QuickPollUserDetailsService class makes use of UserRepository to retrieve User information from the database. It then checks if the retrieved user has administrative rights and constructs an admin GrantedAuthority, namely, ROLE_ADMIN.

The Spring Security infrastructure expects the loadUserByUsername method to return an instance of type UserDetails. Hence, the QuickPollUserDetailsService class creates the o.s.s.c.u.User instance and populates it with the data retrieved from the database. The o.s.s.c.u.User is a concrete implementation of the UserDetails interface. If the QuickPollUserDetailsService can't find a user in the database for the passed-in username, it will throw a UsernameNotFoundException exception.

Customizing Spring Security

Customizing Spring Security's default behavior involves creating a configuration class that is annotated with @EnableWebSecurity. This configuration class typically extends the org.springframework.security.config.annotation.web.configuration. WebSecurityConfigurer class that provides helper methods to simplify our security configuration. Listing 8-9 shows the SecurityConfig class that will contain security-related configuration for QuickPoll application.

Listing 8-9. Security Configuration for QuickPoll

```
package com.apress;

import javax.inject.Inject;
import org.springframework.context.annotation.Configuration;
import org.springframework.security.config.annotation.authentication.
builders.AuthenticationManagerBuilder;
import org.springframework.security.config.annotation.web.configuration.
EnableWebSecurity;
import org.springframework.security.config.annotation.web.configuration.
WebSecurityConfigurerAdapter;
import org.springframework.security.core.userdetails.UserDetailsService;
import org.springframework.security.crypto.bcrypt.BCryptPasswordEncoder;

@Configuration
@EnableWebSecurity
public class SecurityConfig extends WebSecurityConfigurerAdapter {

        @Inject
        private UserDetailsService userDetailsService;
```

```
@Override
protected void configure(AuthenticationManagerBuilder auth) throws
Exception {
        auth.userDetailsService(userDetailsService)
                .passwordEncoder(new BCryptPasswordEncoder());
}
}
```

The SecurityConfig class declares a userDetailsService property, which gets injected with a QuickPollUserDetailsService instance at runtime. It also overrides a super class's configure method that takes an AuthenticationManagerBuilder as parameter. The AuthenticationManagerBuilder is a helper class implementing the Builder pattern that provides an easy way of assembling an AuthenticationManager. In our method implementation, we use the AuthenticationManagerBuilder to add the UserDetailsService instance. Because we have encrypted the passwords stored in the database using BCrypt algorithm, we provide an instance of BCryptPasswordEncoder. The authentication manager framework will use the password encoder to compare the plain string provided by the user with the encrypted hash stored in the database.

With this configuration in place, restart the QuickPoll application and run the following command at the command line:

```
curl -u mickey:cheese http://localhost:8080/v2/polls
```

If you run the command without the -u option and the username/password data, you will receive a 403 error from the server as shown here:

```
{"timestamp":1429998300969,"status":401,"error":"Unauthorized","message":"F
ull authentication is required to access this resource","path":"/v2/polls"}
```

Securing URI

The SecurityConfig class introduced in the previous section gets us one step closer by configuring HTTP Basic authentication to use QuickPoll users. This configuration, however, protects all endpoints and requires authentication to access resources. To implement our requirement to just secure v3 Poll API, we will override another WebSecurityConfigurer's config method. Listing 8-10 shows the config method implementation that needs to be added to the SecurtyConfig class.

Listing 8-10. New Config Method in SecurityConfig

```
import org.springframework.security.config.annotation.web.builders.
HttpSecurity;
import org.springframework.security.config.http.SessionCreationPolicy;

@Override
protected void configure(HttpSecurity http) throws Exception {

        http
          .sessionManagement()
            .sessionCreationPolicy(SessionCreationPolicy.STATELESS)
            .and()
          .authorizeRequests()
            .antMatchers("/v1/**", "/v2/**", "/swagger-ui/**", "/
            api-docs/**").permitAll()
            .antMatchers("/v3/polls/ **").authenticated()
            .and()
          .httpBasic()
            .realmName("Quick Poll")
            .and()
          .csrf()
            .disable();
}
```

The HttpSecurity parameter passed into the config method in Listing 8-10 allows us to specify the URI that should be secured or unsecured. We begin the method implementation by requesting Spring Security to not create an HTTP session and not store logged-in user's SecurityContext in the session. This is achieved using the SessionCreationPolicy.STATELESS creation policy. We then use antMatchers to provide Ant-style URI expressions that we don't want Spring Security protecting. Using the permitAll method, we are specifying that the API versions 1 and 2 and Swagger UI should be available anonymously. The next antMatchers along with authenticated method specifies that Spring Security should only allow authenticated users to access V3 Polls API. Finally, we enable HTTP Basic authentication and set the realm name to "Quick Poll." Restart QuickPoll application and you should be prompted for authentication only on the /v3/polls resources.

> **Note**   Cross-Site Request Forgery, or CSRF (`http://en.wikipedia.org/wiki/Cross-site_request_forgery`), is a type of security vulnerability whereby a malicious website forces the end user to execute unwanted commands on a different website in which they are currently authenticated. Spring Security by default enables CSRF protection and highly recommends using it for requests submitted by a user via a browser. For services that are used by nonbrowser clients, the CSRF can be disabled. By implementing custom `RequestMatchers`, it is possible to disable CSRF only for certain URLs or HTTP methods.
>
> To keep things simple and manageable for this book, we have disabled CSRF protection.

The last security requirement that we have is to ensure that only users with administrative privileges can delete a poll. To implement this authorization requirement, we will apply Spring Security's method level security on the `deletePoll` method. Spring's method level security can be enabled using the aptly named `org.springframework.security.config.annotation.method.configuration.EnableGlobalMethodSecurity` annotation. Listing 8-11 shows the annotation added to the `SecurityConfig` class.

Listing 8-11. EnableGlobalMethodSecurity Annotation Added

```
package com.apress;
import org.springframework.security.config.annotation.method.configuration.
EnableGlobalMethodSecurity;

@Configuration
@EnableWebSecurity
@EnableGlobalMethodSecurity(prePostEnabled = true)
public class SecurityConfig extends WebMvcConfigurer {
        // Content removed for brevity
}
```

Spring Security supports a rich set of class and method-level authorization annotations along with standard-based JSR 250 annotation security. The `prePostEnabled` flag in `EnableGlobalMethodSecurity` requests Spring Security to enable annotations that perform pre- and post-method invocation authorization checks. The next step is to annotate the v3 PollController's deletePoll method with @ PreAuthorize annotation as shown in Listing 8-12.

Listing 8-12. PreAuthorize Annotation Added

```
import org.springframework.security.access.prepost.PreAuthorize;

@PreAuthorize("hasAuthority('ROLE_ADMIN')")
public ResponseEntity<Void> deletePoll(@PathVariable Long pollId) {
        // Code removed for brevity
}
```

The @PreAuthorize annotation decides if the deletePoll method can be invoked or not. Spring Security makes this decision by evaluating the Spring-EL expression passed in as the annotation's value. In this case, the hasAuthority checks if the logged-in user has the "ROLE_ADMIN" authority. Restart the application and perform a DELETE on the endpoint http://localhost:8080/v3/polls/12 using Postman. When prompted for credentials, enter the username mickey and the password cheese, and hit Log In. Figure 8-8 shows the request and associated inputs.

Figure 8-8. *Deleting poll with unauthorized users*

Since the user mickey doesn't have administrative rights, you will see an unauthorized response from the service, as shown in Figure 8-9.

Figure 8-9. *Unauthorized delete response*

Now let's retry this request using an admin user with administrative rights. In Postman, click the Basic Auth tab and enter the credentials admin/admin and hit "Refresh headers" as shown in Figure 8-10. On submitting the request, you should see the Poll resource with ID 12 deleted.

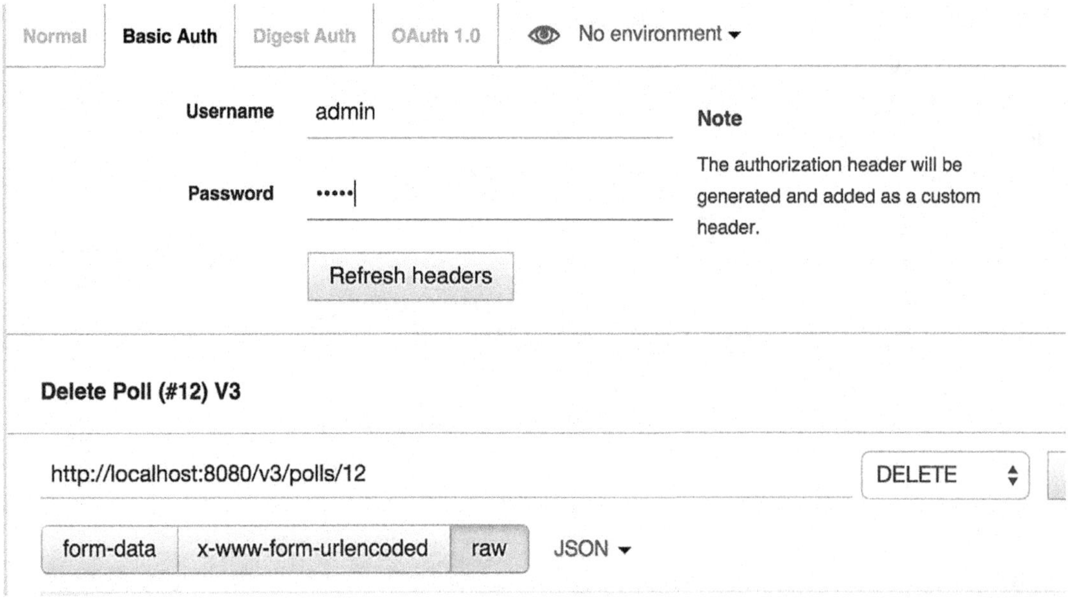

Figure 8-10. *Basic Auth admin credentials in Postman*

To delete a Poll using cURL, run the following command:

```
curl -i -u admin:admin  -X DELETE http://localhost:3/v3/polls/13
```

The previously mentioned command deletes a Poll resource with ID 13. The -i option requests curl to output the response headers. The -X option allows us to specify the HTTP method name. In our case, we specified the DELETE HTTP method. The output of this result is shown in Listing 8-13.

Listing 8-13. Output of cURL Delete

```
HTTP/1.1 200 OK
Server: Apache-Coyote/1.1
X-Content-Type-Options: nosniff
X-XSS-Protection: 1; mode=block
Cache-Control: no-cache, no-store, max-age=0, must-revalidate
Pragma: no-cache
Expires: 0
X-Frame-Options: DENY
Content-Length: 0
Date: Sat, 25 Apr 2015 21:50:35 GMT
```

Summary

Security is an important aspect of any enterprise application. In this chapter, we reviewed strategies for securing REST services. We also took a deeper look into OAuth 2 and reviewed its different components. We then used Spring Security to implement Basic authentication in our QuickPoll application. In the next chapter, we will use Spring's RestTemplate to build REST clients. We will also use the Spring MVC Test framework to perform unit and integration testing on REST controllers.

CHAPTER 9

Clients and Testing

In this chapter we will discuss the following:

- Building clients using RestTemplate

- Spring Test framework basics

- Unit testing MVC controllers

- Integration testing MVC controllers

We have looked at building REST services using Spring. In this chapter, we will look at building clients that consume these REST services. We will also examine the Spring Test framework that can be used to perform unit and end-to-end testing of REST services.

QuickPoll Java Client

Consuming REST services involves building a JSON or XML request payload, transmitting the payload via HTTP/HTTPS, and consuming the returned JSON response. This flexibility opens doors to numerous options for building REST clients in Java (or, as a matter of fact, any technology). A straightforward approach for building a Java REST client is to use core JDK libraries. Listing 9-1 shows an example of a client reading a Poll using the QuickPoll REST API.

Listing 9-1. Reading a Poll Using Java URLClass

```
public void readPoll() {
        HttpURLConnection connection = null;
        BufferedReader reader = null;
        try {
```

© Balaji Varanasi and Maxim Bartkov 2022
B. Varanasi and M. Bartkov, *Spring REST*, https://doi.org/10.1007/978-1-4842-7477-4_9

```
            URL restAPIUrl = new URL("http://localhost:8080/v1/
            polls/1");
            connection = (HttpURLConnection) restAPIUrl.
            openConnection();
            connection.setRequestMethod("GET");

            // Read the response

reader = new BufferedReader(new InputStreamReader(connection.
getInputStream()));
            StringBuilder jsonData = new StringBuilder();
            String line;
            while ((line = reader.readLine()) != null) {
                    jsonData.append(line);
            }

            System.out.println(jsonData.toString());
        }
        catch(Exception e) {
                e.printStackTrace();
        }
        finally {
                // Clean up
                IOUtils.closeQuietly(reader);
                if(connection != null)
                        connection.disconnect();

        }
}
```

Although there is nothing wrong with the approach in Listing 9-1, there is a lot of boilerplate code that needs to be written to perform a simple REST operation. The readPoll method would grow even bigger if we were to include the code to parse the JSON response. Spring abstracts this boilerplate code into templates and utility classes and makes it easy to consume REST services.

RestTemplate

Central to Spring's support for building REST clients is the org.springframework.web.
client.RestTemplate. The RestTemplate takes care of the necessary plumbing needed
to communicate with REST services and automatically marshals/unmarshals HTTP
request and response bodies. The RestTemplate like Spring's other popular helper
classes such as JdbcTemplate and JmsTemplate is based on the Template Method design
pattern.[1]

The RestTemplate and associated utility classes are part of the spring-web.jar file.
If you are building a standalone REST client using RestTemplate, you need to add the
spring-web dependency, shown in Listing 9-2, to your pom.xml file.

Listing 9-2. Spring-web.jar Dependency

```
<dependency>
  <groupId>org.springframework</groupId>
  <artifactId>spring-web</artifactId>
  <version>5.3.9</version>
</dependency>
```

RestTemplate provides convenient methods to perform API requests using six
commonly used HTTP methods. In the next sections, we will look at some of these
functions along with a generic yet powerful exchange method to build QuickPoll clients.

Note   In this chapter we will continue building on the work that we did on the
QuickPoll application in the previous chapters. Alternatively, a starter project inside
the Chapter9\starter folder of the downloaded source code is available for
you to use. The completed solution is available under the Chapter9\final folder.
Please refer to this solution for complete listings containing getters/setters and
additional imports.

---

[1]http://en.wikipedia.org/wiki/Template_method_pattern.

Getting Polls

RestTemplate provides a getForObject method to retrieve representations using the GET HTTP method. Listing 9-3 shows the three flavors of the getForObject method.

Listing 9-3. GetForObject Method Flavors

```
public <T> T getForObject(String url, Class<T> responseType, Object...
urlVariables) throws  RestClientException {}
public <T> T getForObject(String url, Class<T> responseType, Map<String,?>
urlVariables) throws RestClientException
public <T> T getForObject(URI url, Class<T> responseType) throws
RestClientException
```

The first two methods accept a URI template string, a return value type, and URI variables that can be used to expand the URI template. The third flavor accepts a fully formed URI and return value type. RestTemplate encodes the passed-in URI templates, and, hence, if the URI is already encoded, you must use the third method flavor. Otherwise, it will result in double encoding of the URI, causing malformed URI errors.

Listing 9-4 shows the QuickPollClient class and the usage of getForObject method to retrieve a Poll for a given poll id. The QuickPollClient is placed under the com.apress.client package of our QuickPoll application and is interacting with the first version of our QuickPoll API. In the upcoming sections, we will create clients that interact with second and third versions of the API. RestTemplate is threadsafe, and, hence, we created a class-level RestTemplate instance to be used by all client methods. Because we have specified the Poll.class as the second parameter, RestTemplate uses HTTP message converters and automatically converts the HTTP response content into a Poll instance.

Listing 9-4. QuickPollClient and GetForObject Usage

```
package com.apress.client;

import org.springframework.web.client.RestTemplate;
import com.apress.domain.Poll;

public class QuickPollClient {
```

```
        private static final String QUICK_POLL_URI_V1 = "http://
        localhost:8080/v1/polls";
        private RestTemplate restTemplate = new RestTemplate();

        public Poll getPollById(Long pollId) {
return restTemplate.getForObject(QUICK_POLL_URI_V1 + "/{pollId}", Poll.
class, pollId);
        }
}
```

This listing demonstrates the power of RestTemplate. It took about a dozen lines in Listing 9-1, but we were able to accomplish that and more with a couple of lines using RestTemplate. The getPollById method can be tested with a simple main method in QuickPollClient class:

```
public static void main(String[] args) {
        QuickPollClient client = new QuickPollClient();
        Poll poll = client.getPollById(1L);
        System.out.println(poll);
}
```

Note   Ensure that you have the QuickPoll application up and running before you run the main method.

Retrieving a Poll collection resource is a little trickier as providing List<Poll>. class as a return value type to the getForObject would result in compilation error. One approach is to simply specify that we are expecting a collection:

```
List allPolls =  restTemplate.getForObject(QUICK_POLL_URI_V1, List.class);
```

However, because RestTemplate can't automatically guess the Java class type of the elements, it would deserialize each JSON object in the returned collection into a LinkedHashMap. Hence, the call returns all of our Polls as a collection of type List<LinkedHashMap>.

To address this issue, Spring provides a `org.springframework.core.` `ParameterizedTypeReference` abstract class that can capture and retain generic-type information at runtime. So, to specify the fact that we are expecting a list of Poll instances, we create a subclass of `ParameterizedTypeReference`:

```
ParameterizedTypeReference<List<Poll>> responseType = new ParameterizedType
Reference<List<Poll>>() {};
```

RestTemplate HTTP-specific methods such as getForObject don't take a ParameterizedTypeReference as their parameter. As shown in Listing 9-5, we need to use RestTemplate's exchange method in conjunction with ParameterizedTypeReference. The exchange method infers the return-type information from the passed-in responseType parameter and returns a ResponseEntity instance. Invoking the getBody method on ResponseEntity gives us the Poll collection.

Listing 9-5. Get All Polls Using RestTemplate

```
import org.springframework.core.ParameterizedTypeReference;
import org.springframework.http.ResponseEntity;
import org.springframework.http.HttpMethod;

public List<Poll> getAllPolls() {

ParameterizedTypeReference<List<Poll>> responseType = new
ParameterizedTypeReference
<List<Poll>>() {};

ResponseEntity<List<Poll>> responseEntity = restTemplate.exchange(QUICK_
POLL_URI_V1, HttpMethod.GET, null, responseType);
        List<Poll> allPolls = responseEntity.getBody();

        return allPolls;
}
```

We can also accomplish similar behavior with getForObject by requesting RestTemplate to return an array of Poll instances:

```
Poll[] allPolls = restTemplate.getForObject(QUICK_POLL_URI_V1, Poll[].
class);
```

Creating a Poll

RestTemplate provides two methods—postForLocation and postForObject—to perform HTTP POST operations on a resource. Listing 9-6 gives the API for the two methods.

Listing 9-6. RestTemplate's POST Support

```
public URI postForLocation(String url, Object request, Object...
urlVariables) throws RestClientException
public <T> T postForObject(String url, Object request, Class<T>
responseType, Object... uriVariables) throws RestClientException
```

The postForLocation method performs an HTTP POST on the given URI and returns the value of the Location header. As we have seen in our QuickPoll POST implementations, the Location header contains the URI of the newly created resource. The postForObject works similar to postForLocation but converts a response into a representation. The responseType parameter indicates the type of representation to be expected.

Listing 9-7 shows the QuickPollClient's createPoll method that creates a new Poll using the postForLocation method.

Listing 9-7. Create a Poll Using PostForLocation

```
public URI createPoll(Poll poll) {
        return restTemplate.postForLocation( QUICK_POLL_URI_V1, poll);
}
```

Update the QuickPollClient's main method with this code to test the createPoll method:

```
public static void main(String[] args) {
        QuickPollClient client = new QuickPollClient();

        Poll newPoll = new Poll();
        newPoll.setQuestion("What is your favourite color?");
        Set<Option> options = new HashSet<>();
        newPoll.setOptions(options);
```

```
Option option1 = new Option(); option1.setValue("Red"); options.
add(option1);
Option option2 = new Option(); option2.setValue("Blue");options.
add(option2);

URI pollLocation = client.createPoll(newPoll);
System.out.println("Newly Created Poll Location " + pollLocation);
}
```

PUT Method

The RestTemplate provides the aptly named PUT method to support the PUT HTTP method. Listing 9-8 shows QuickPollClient's updatePoll method that updates a poll instance. Notice that the PUT method doesn't return any response and communicates failures by throwing RestClientException or its subclasses.

Listing 9-8. Update a Poll Using PUT

```
public void updatePoll(Poll poll) {
        restTemplate.put(QUICK_POLL_URI_V1 + "/{pollId}",  poll, poll.
        getId());
}
```

DELETE Method

The RestTemplate provides three overloaded DELETE methods to support DELETE HTTP operations. The DELETE methods follow semantics similar to PUT and don't return a value. They communicate any exceptions via RestClientException or its subclasses. Listing 9-9 shows the deletePoll method implementation in QuickPollClient class.

Listing 9-9. Delete a Poll

```
public void deletePoll(Long pollId) {
        restTemplate.delete(QUICK_POLL_URI_V1 + "/{pollId}",  pollId);
}
```

Handling Pagination

In version 2 of our QuickPoll API, we introduced paging. So, the clients upgrading to version 2 need to re-implement the getAllPolls method. All other client methods will remain unchanged.

To re-implement the getAllPolls, our first instinct would be to simply pass the org. springframework.data.domain.PageImpl as the parameterized type reference:

```
ParameterizedTypeReference<PageImpl<Poll>> responseType = new Parameterized
TypeReference<PageImpl<Poll>>() {};
ResponseEntity<PageImpl<Poll>> responseEntity = restTemplate.
exchange(QUICK_POLL_URI_2, HttpMethod.GET, null, responseType);
PageImpl<Poll> allPolls = responseEntity.getBody();
```

The PageImpl is a concrete implementation of the org.springframework.data. domain.Page interface and can hold all of the paging and sorting information returned by the QuickPoll REST API. The only problem with this approach is that PageImpl doesn't have a default constructor and Spring's HTTP message converter would fail with the following exception:

```
Could not read JSON: No suitable constructor found for type [simple type,
class org.springframework.data.domain.PageImpl<com.apress.domain.Poll>]:
can not instantiate from JSON object (need to add/enable type information?)
```

To handle pagination and successfully map JSON to an object, we will create a Java class that mimics PageImpl class but also has a default constructor, as shown in Listing 9-10.

Listing 9-10. PageWrapper Class

```
package com.apress.client;

import java.util.List;
import org.springframework.data.domain.Sort;

public class PageWrapper<T> {
        private List<T> content;

        private Boolean last;
        private Boolean first;
```

```
private Integer totalPages;
private Integer totalElements;
private Integer size;
private Integer number;
private Integer numberOfElements;
private Sort sort;

// Getters and Setters removed for brevity
}
```

Note   There are occasions when you need to generate Java types from JSON. This is especially true for APIs that don't provide a Java client library. The online tool `www.jsonschema2pojo.org` provides a convenient way to generate Java POJOs from JSON schema or JSON data.

The `PageWrapper` class can hold the returned content and has attributes to hold the paging information. Listing 9-11 shows the `QuickPollClientV2` class that makes use of `PageWrapper` to interact with second version of API. Notice that the `getAllPolls` method now takes two parameters: `page` and `size`. The `page` parameter determines the requested page number, and the `size` parameter determines the number of elements to be included in the page. This implementation can be further enhanced to accept sort parameters and provide sorting functionality.

Listing 9-11. QuickPoll Client for Version 2

```
package com.apress.client;
import org.springframework.core.ParameterizedTypeReference;
import org.springframework.http.HttpMethod;
import org.springframework.http.ResponseEntity;
import org.springframework.web.client.RestTemplate;
import org.springframework.web.util.UriComponentsBuilder;
import com.apress.domain.Poll;
```

```
public class QuickPollClientV2 {
        private static final String QUICK_POLL_URI_2 = "http://
        localhost:8080/v2/polls";
        private RestTemplate restTemplate = new RestTemplate();

        public PageWrapper<Poll> getAllPolls(int page, int size) {

ParameterizedTypeReference<PageWrapper<Poll>> responseType = new
ParameterizedTypeReference<PageWrapper<Poll>>() {};
                UriComponentsBuilder builder = UriComponentsBuilder
                                                .fromHttpUrl(QUICK_POLL_
                                                URI_2)
                                                .queryParam("page", page)
                                                .queryParam("size", size);

ResponseEntity<PageWrapper<Poll>> responseEntity = restTemplate.exchange
(builder.build().toUri(), HttpMethod.GET, null, responseType);
                return responseEntity.getBody();
        }
}
```

Handling Basic Authentication

Up to this point we have created clients for the first and second versions of QuickPoll API. In Chapter 8, we secured the third version of the API, and any communication with that version requires Basic authentication. For example, running a DELETE method on URI http://localhost:8080/v3/polls/3 without any authentication would result in an HttpClientErrorException with a 401 status code.

To successfully interact with our QuickPoll v3 API, we need to programmatically base 64 encode a user's credentials and construct an authorization request header. Listing 9-12 shows such implementation: we concatenate the passed-in username and password. We then base 64 encode it and create an Authorization header by prefixing Basic to the encoded value.

Listing 9-12. Authentication Header Implementation

```
import org.apache.tomcat.util.codec.binary.Base64;
import org.springframework.http.HttpHeaders;

private HttpHeaders getAuthenticationHeader(String username, String
password) {
        String credentials = username + ":" + password;
        byte[] base64CredentialData = Base64.encodeBase64(credentials.
        getBytes());

        HttpHeaders headers = new HttpHeaders();
        headers.set("Authorization", "Basic " + new
        String(base64CredentialData));
        return headers;
}
```

The RestTemplate's exchange method can be used to perform an HTTP operation and takes in an Authorization header. Listing 9-13 shows the QuickPollClientV3BasicAuth class with deletePoll method implementation using Basic authentication.

Listing 9-13. QuickPoll Client with Basic Auth

```
package com.apress.client;

import org.springframework.http.HttpHeaders;
import org.springframework.http.HttpMethod;
import org.springframework.web.client.RestTemplate;
import org.springframework.http.HttpEntity;

public class QuickPollClientV3BasicAuth {
        private static final String QUICK_POLL_URI_V3 = "http://
        localhost:8080/v3/polls";
        private RestTemplate restTemplate = new RestTemplate();

        public void deletePoll(Long pollId) {
```

```
HttpHeaders authenticationHeaders = getAuthenticationHeader("admin", "admin");
            restTemplate.exchange(QUICK_POLL_URI_V3 + "/{pollId}",

HttpMethod.DELETE, new HttpEntity<Void>(authenticationHeaders),
Void.class, pollId);
        }
}
```

Note   In this approach, we have manually set the Authentication header to each request. Another approach is to implement a custom `ClientHttpRequestInterceptor` that intercepts each outgoing request and automatically appends the header to it.

Testing REST Services

Testing is an important aspect of every software development process. Testing comes in different flavors, and in this chapter, we will focus on unit and integration testing. Unit testing verifies that individual, isolated *units* of code are working as expected. It is the most common type of testing that developers typically perform. Integration testing typically follows unit testing and focuses on the interaction between previously tested units.

The Java ecosystem is filled with frameworks that ease unit and integration testing. JUnit and TestNG have become the de facto standard test frameworks and provide foundation/integration to most other testing frameworks. Although Spring supports both frameworks, we will be using JUnit in this book, as it is familiar to most readers.

Spring Test

The Spring Framework provides the `spring-test` module that allows you to integrate Spring into tests. The module provides a rich set of annotations, utility classes, and mock objects for environment JNDI, Servlet, and Portlet API. The framework also provides capabilities to cache application context across test executions to improve performance.

Using this infrastructure, you can easily inject Spring beans and test fixtures into tests. To use the spring-test module in a non–Spring Boot project, you need to include the Maven dependency as shown in Listing 9-14.

Listing 9-14. Spring-test Dependency

```
<dependency>
        <groupId>org.springframework</groupId>
        <artifactId>spring-test</artifactId>
        <version>3.5.9</version>
        <scope>test</scope>
</dependency>
```

Spring Boot provides a starter POM named `spring-boot-starter-test` that automatically adds the `spring-test` module to a Boot application. Additionally, the starter POM brings in JUnit, Mockito, and Hamcrest libraries:

- Mockito is a popular mocking framework for Java. It provides a simple and easy-to-use API to create and configure mocks. More details about Mockito can be found at `http://mockito.org/`.

- Hamcrest is a framework that provides a powerful vocabulary for creating matchers. To put it simply, a matcher allows you to match an object against a set of expectations. Matchers improve the way that we write assertions by making them more human readable. They also generate meaningful failure messages when assertions are not met during testing. You can learn more about Hamcrest at `http://hamcrest.org/`.

To understand the `spring-test` module, let's examine a typical test case. Listing 9-15 shows a sample test built using JUnit and `spring-test` infrastructure.

Listing 9-15. Sample JUnit Test

```
@RunWith(SpringJUnit4ClassRunner.class)
@SpringBootTest(classes = QuickPollApplication.class)
@WebAppConfiguration
public class ExampleTest {
        @Before
        public void setup() { }
```

```
@Test
public void testSomeThing() {}

@After
public void teardown() { }
}
```

Our example test contains three methods—setup, testSomeThing, and teardown each annotated with a JUnit annotation. The @Test annotation denotes the testSomeThing as a JUnit test method. This method will contain code that ensures our production code works as expected. The @Before annotation instructs JUnit to run the setup method prior to any test method execution. Methods annotated with @Before can be used for setting up test fixtures and test data. Similarly, the @After annotation instructs JUnit to run the teardown method after any test method execution. Methods annotated with @After are typically used to tear down test fixtures and perform cleanup operations.

JUnit uses the notion of test runner to perform test execution. By default, JUnit uses the BlockJUnit4ClassRunner test runner to execute test methods and associated life cycle (@Before or @After, etc.) methods. The @RunWith annotation allows you to alter this behavior. In our example, using the @RunWith annotation, we are instructing JUnit to use the SpringJUnit4ClassRunner class to run the test cases.

The SpringJUnit4ClassRunner adds Spring integration by performing activities such as loading application context, injecting autowired dependencies, and running specified test execution listeners. For Spring to load and configure an application context, it needs the locations of the XML context files or the names of the Java configuration classes. We typically use the @ContextConfiguration annotation to provide this information to the SpringJUnit4ClassRunner class.

In our example, however, we use the SpringBootTest, a specialized version of the standard ContextConfiguration that provides additional Spring Boot features. Finally, the @WebAppConfiguration annotation instructs Spring to create the web version of the application context, namely, WebApplicationContext.

Unit Testing REST Controllers

Spring's dependency injection makes unit testing easier. Dependencies can be easily mocked or simulated with predefined behavior, thereby allowing us to zoom in and test code in isolation. Traditionally, unit testing Spring MVC controllers followed this paradigm. For example, Listing 9-16 shows the code unit testing PollController's getAllPolls method.

Listing 9-16. Unit Testing PollController with Mocks

```
import static org.junit.Assert.assertEquals;
import static org.mockito.Mockito.when;
import static org.mockito.Mockito.times;
import static org.mockito.Mockito.verify;
import java.util.ArrayList;
import com.google.common.collect.Lists;
import org.junit.Before;
import org.junit.Test;
import org.mockito.Mock;
import org.mockito.MockitoAnnotations;
import org.springframework.http.HttpStatus;
import org.springframework.http.ResponseEntity;
import org.springframework.test.util.ReflectionTestUtils;

public class PollControllerTestMock {
	@Mock
	private PollRepository pollRepository;

	@Before
	public void setUp() throws Exception {
		MockitoAnnotations.initMocks(this);
	}

	@Test
	public void testGetAllPolls() {
		PollController pollController  = new PollController();
```

```
ReflectionTestUtils.setField(pollController, "pollRepository",
pollRepository);

                when(pollRepository.findAll()).thenReturn(new
                ArrayList<Poll>());

ResponseEntity<Iterable<Poll>> allPollsEntity = pollController.
getAllPolls();
                verify(pollRepository, times(1)).findAll();
                assertEquals(HttpStatus.OK, allPollsEntity.
                getStatusCode());
                assertEquals(0, Lists.newArrayList(allPollsEntity.
                getBody()).size());
        }

}
```

The `PollControllerTestMock` implementation uses the `Mockito`'s `@Mock` annotation to mock `PollController`'s only dependency: `PollRepository`. For Mockito to properly initialize the annotated `pollRepository` property, we either need to run the test using the `MockitoJUnitRunner` test runner or invoke the `initMocks` method in the `MockitoAnnotations`. In our test, we choose the latter approach and call the `initMocks` in the `@Before` method.

In the `testGetAllPolls` method, we create an instance of `PollController` and inject the mock `PollRepository` using Spring's `ReflectionTestUtils` utility class. Then we use Mockito's `when` and `thenReturn` methods to set the `PollRepository` mock's behavior. Here are we indicating that when the `PollRepository`'s `findAll()` method is invoked, an empty collection should be returned. Finally, we invoke the `getAllPolls` method and verify `findAll()` method's invocation and assert controller's return value.

In this strategy, we treat the `PollController` as a POJO and hence don't test the controller's request mappings, validations, data bindings, and any associated exception handlers. Starting from version 3.2, `spring-test` module includes a Spring MVC Test framework that allows us to test a controller as a controller. This test framework will load the `DispatcherServlet` and associated web components such as controllers and view resolvers into test context. It then uses the `DispatcherServlet` to process all the requests and generates responses as if it is running in a web container without actually starting up a web server. This allows us to perform a more thorough testing of Spring MVC applications.

Spring MVC Test Framework Basics

To gain a better understanding of the Spring MVC Test framework, we explore its four important classes: MockMvc, MockMvcRequestBuilders, MockMvcResultMatchers, and MockMvcBuilders. As evident from the class names, the Spring MVC Test framework makes heavy use of Builder pattern.[2]

Central to the test framework is the org.springframework.test.web.servlet. MockMvc class, which can be used to perform HTTP requests. It contains only one method named perform and has the following API signature:

```
public ResultActions perform(RequestBuilder requestBuilder) throws java.
lang.Exception
```

The RequestBuilder parameter provides an abstraction to create the request (GET, POST, etc.) to be executed. To simplify request construction, the framework provides an org.springframework.test.web.servlet.request.MockHttpServletRequestBuilder implementation and a set of helper static methods in the org.springframework.test. web.servlet.request.MockMvcRequestBuilders class. Listing 9-17 gives an example of a POST HTTP request constructed using the previously mentioned classes.

Listing 9-17. POST HTTP Request

```
post("/test_uri")
 .param("admin", "false")
 .accept(MediaType.APPLICATION_JSON)
 .content("{JSON_DATA}");
```

The post method is part of the MockMvcRequestBuilders class and is used to create a POST request. The MockMvcRequestBuilders also provides additional methods such as get, delete, and put to create corresponding HTTP requests. The param method is part of the MockHttpServletRequestBuilder class and is used to add a parameter to the request. The MockHttpServletRequestBuilder provides additional methods such as accept, content, cookie, and header to add data and metadata to the request being constructed.

---

[2] http://en.wikipedia.org/wiki/Builder_pattern.

The `perform` method returns an `org.springframework.test.web.servlet.` `ResultActions` instance that can be used to apply assertions/expectations on the executed response. Listing 9-18 shows three assertions applied to the response of a sample POST request using `ResultActions`'s `andExpect` method. The `status` is a static method in `org.springframework.test.web.servlet.result.MockMvcResultMatchers` that allows you to apply assertions on response status. Its `isOk` method asserts that the status code is 200 (HTTPStatus.OK). Similarly, the `content` method in `MockMvcResultMatchers` provides methods to assert response body. Here we are asserting that the response content type is of type "application/json" and matches an expected string "`JSON_DATA.`"

Listing 9-18. ResultActions

```
mockMvc.perform(post("/test_uri"))
       .andExpect(status().isOk())
       .andExpect(content().contentType(MediaType.APPLICATION_JSON))
       .andExpect(content().string("{JSON_DATA}"));
```

So far, we have looked at using `MockMvc` to perform requests and assert the response. Before we can use `MockMvc`, we need to initialize it. The `MockMvcBuilders` class provides the following two methods to build a `MockMvc` instance:

- `WebAppContextSetup`—Builds a `MockMvc` instance using a fully initialized `WebApplicationContext`. The entire Spring configuration associated with the context is loaded before `MockMvc` instance is created. This technique is used for end-to-end testing.

- `StandaloneSetup`—Builds a `MockMvc` without loading any Spring configuration. Only the basic MVC infrastructure is loaded for testing controllers. This technique is used for unit testing.

Unit Testing Using Spring MVC Test Framework

Now that we have reviewed the Spring MVC Test framework, let's look at using it to test REST controllers. The `PollControllerTest` class in Listing 9-19 demonstrates testing the `getPolls` method. To the `@ContextConfiguration` annotation, we pass in a `MockServletContext` class instructing Spring to set up an empty

WebApplicationContext. An empty WebApplicationContext allows us to instantiate and initialize the one controller that we want to test without loading up the entire application context. It also allows us to mock the dependencies that the controller requires.

Listing 9-19. Unit Testing with Spring MVC Test

```
package com.apress.unit;

import static org.mockito.Mockito.when;
import static org.springframework.test.web.servlet.request.
MockMvcRequestBuilders.get;
import static org.springframework.test.web.servlet.result.
MockMvcResultMatchers.content;
import static org.springframework.test.web.servlet.result.
MockMvcResultMatchers.status;
import static org.springframework.test.web.servlet.setup.MockMvcBuilders.
standaloneSetup;
import org.mockito.InjectMocks;
import org.mockito.Mock;
import org.mockito.MockitoAnnotations;
import org.springframework.boot.test.context.SpringBootTest;
import org.springframework.mock.web.MockServletContext;
import org.springframework.test.web.servlet.MockMvc;

@RunWith(SpringJUnit4ClassRunner.class)
@SpringBootTest(classes = QuickPollApplication.class)
@ContextConfiguration(classes = MockServletContext.class)
@WebAppConfiguration
public class PollControllerTest {

        @InjectMocks
        PollController pollController;

        @Mock
        private PollRepository pollRepository;

        private MockMvc mockMvc;
```

```
@Before
public void setUp() throws Exception {
        MockitoAnnotations.initMocks(this);
        mockMvc = standaloneSetup(pollController).build();
}

@Test
public void testGetAllPolls() throws Exception {
        when(pollRepository.findAll()).thenReturn(new
        ArrayList<Poll>());
        mockMvc.perform(get("/v1/polls"))
                .andExpect(status().isOk())
                .andExpect(content().string("[]"));
}
}
```

In this case, we want to test version 1 of our PollController API. So we declare a pollController property and annotate it with @InjectMocks. During runtime, Mockito sees the @InjectMocks annotation and will create an instance of the import com. apress.v1.controller.PollController.PollController. It then injects it with any mocks declared in the PollControllerTest class using constructor/field or setter injection. The only mock we have in the class is the PollRepository.

In the @Before annotated method, we use the MockMvcBuilders's standaloneSetup() method to register the pollController instance. The standaloneSetup() automatically creates the minimum infrastructure required by the DispatcherServlet to serve requests associated with the registered controllers. The MockMvc instance built by standaloneSetup is stored in a class-level variable and made available to tests.

In the testGetAllPolls method, we use Mockito to program the PollRepository mock's behavior. Then we perform a GET request on the /v1/polls URI and use the status and content assertions to ensure that an empty JSON array is returned. This is the biggest difference from the version that we saw in Listing 9-16. There we were testing the result of a Java method invocation. Here we are testing the HTTP response that the API generates.

Integration Testing REST Controllers

In the previous section, we looked at unit testing a controller and its associated configuration. However, this testing is limited to a web layer. There are times when we want to test all of the layers of an application from controllers to the persistent store. In the past, writing such tests required launching the application in an embedded Tomcat or Jetty server and use a framework such as HtmlUnit or RestTemplate to trigger HTTP requests. Depending on an external servlet container can be cumbersome and often slows down testing.

The Spring MVC Test framework provides a lightweight, out-of-the-container alternative for integration testing MVC applications. In this approach, the entire Spring application context along with the DispatcherServlet and associated MVC infrastructure gets loaded. A mocked MVC container is made available to receive and execute HTTP requests. We interact with real controllers and these controllers work with real collaborators. To speed up integration testing, complex services are sometimes mocked. Additionally, the context is usually configured such that the DAO/repository layer interacts with an in-memory database.

This approach is similar to the approach we used for unit testing controllers, except for these three differences:

- The entire Spring context gets loaded as opposed to an empty context in the unit testing case.

- All REST endpoints are available as opposed to the ones configured via standaloneSetup.

- Tests are performed using real collaborators against in-memory database as opposed to mocking dependency's behavior.

An integration test for the PollController's getAllPolls method is shown in Listing 9-20. The PollControllerIT class is similar to the PollControllerTest that we looked at earlier. A fully configured instance of WebApplicationContext is injected into the test. In the @Before method, we use this WebApplicationContext instance to build a MockMvc instance using MockMvcBuilders's webAppContextSetup.

Listing 9-20. Integration Testing with Spring MVC Test

```
package com.apress.it;

import static org.hamcrest.Matchers.hasSize;
import static org.springframework.test.web.servlet.request.
MockMvcRequestBuilders.get;
import static org.springframework.test.web.servlet.result.
MockMvcResultMatchers.jsonPath;
import static org.springframework.test.web.servlet.result.
MockMvcResultMatchers.status;
import static org.springframework.test.web.servlet.setup.MockMvcBuilders.
webAppContextSetup;
import org.springframework.boot.test.context.SpringBootTest;
import org.springframework.test.context.junit4.SpringJUnit4ClassRunner;
import org.springframework.test.context.web.WebAppConfiguration;
import org.springframework.test.web.servlet.MockMvc;
import org.springframework.web.context.WebApplicationContext;
import com.apress.QuickPollApplication;

@RunWith(SpringJUnit4ClassRunner.class)
@SpringBootTest(classes = QuickPollApplication.class)
@WebAppConfiguration
public class PollControllerIT {

        @Inject
        private WebApplicationContext webApplicationContext;

        private MockMvc mockMvc;

        @Before
        public void setup() {
                mockMvc = webAppContextSetup(webApplicationContext).build();
        }
```

```
    @Test
    public void testGetAllPolls() throws Exception {
            mockMvc.perform(get("/v1/polls"))
                    .andExpect(status().isOk())
                    .andExpect(jsonPath("$", hasSize(20)));
    }
}
```

The testGetAllPolls method implementation uses the MockMvc instance to perform a GET request on the /v1/polls endpoint. We use two assertions to ensure that the result is what we expect:

- The isOK assertion ensures that we get a status code 200.

- The JsonPath method allows us to write assertions against response body using JsonPath expression. The JsonPath (http://goessner. net/articles/JsonPath/) provides a convenient way to extract parts of a JSON document. To put it simply, JsonPath is to JSON is what XPath is to XML.

In our test case, we use the Hamcrest's hasSize matcher to assert that the retuned JSON contains 20 polls. The import.sql script used to populate the in-memory database contains 20 poll entries. Hence, our assertion uses the magic number 20 for comparison.

Summary

Spring provides powerful template and utility classes that simplify REST client development. In this chapter, we reviewed RestTemplate and used it to perform client operations such as GET, POST, PUT, and DELETE on resources. We also reviewed the Spring MVC Test framework and its core classes. Finally, we used the test framework to simplify unit and integration test creation.

CHAPTER 10

HATEOAS

In this chapter we will discuss the following:

- HATEOAS
- JSON hypermedia types
- QuickPoll HATEOAS implementation

Consider any interaction with an ecommerce website such as Amazon.com. You typically begin your interaction by visiting the site's home page. The home page might contain texts, images, and videos describing different products and promotions. The page also contains hyperlinks that allow you to navigate from one page to another, allow you to read product details and reviews, and allow you to add products to shopping carts. These hyperlinks along with other controls such as buttons and input fields also guide you through workflows such as checking out an order.

Each web page in the workflow presents you with controls to go to the next step or go back to a previous step or even completely exit the workflow. This is a very powerful feature of the Web—you as a consumer use links to navigate through resources finding what you need without having to remember all of their corresponding URIs. You just needed to know the initial URI: `http://www.amazon.com`. If Amazon were to go through a rebranding exercise and change its URIs for products or add new steps in its checkout workflow, you will still be able to discover and perform all the operations.

In this chapter we will review HATEOAS, a constraint that allows us to build resilient REST services that function like a website.

© Balaji Varanasi and Maxim Bartkov 2022
B. Varanasi and M. Bartkov, *Spring REST*, https://doi.org/10.1007/978-1-4842-7477-4_10

HATEOAS

The **H**ypermedia **A**s **T**he **E**ngine **O**f **A**pplication **S**tate, or HATEOAS, is a key constraint of REST architecture. The term "hypermedia" refers to any content that contains links to other forms of media such as images, movies, and texts. As you have experienced, the Web is a classic example of hypermedia. The idea behind HATEOAS is simple—a response would include links to other resources. Clients would use these links to interact with the server, and these interactions could result in possible state changes.

Similar to a human's interaction with a website, a REST client hits an initial API URI and uses the server-provided links to dynamically discover available actions and access the resources it needs. The client need not have prior knowledge of the service or the different steps involved in a workflow. Additionally, the clients no longer have to hard-code the URI structures for different resources. This allows the server to make URI changes as the API evolves without breaking the clients.

To better understand HATEOAS, consider REST API for a hypothetical blog application. An example request to retrieve a blog post resource with identifier 1 and the associated response in JSON format is shown here:

```
GET     /posts/1        HTTP/1.1
Connection: keep-alive
Host: blog.example.com
```

```
{
        "id" : 1,
        "body" : "My first blog post",
        "postdate" : "2015-05-30T21:41:12.650Z"
}
```

As we would expect, the generated response from the server contains the data associated with the blog post resource. When a HATEOAS constraint is applied to this REST service, the generated response has links embedded in it. Listing 10-1 shows an example response with links.

Listing 10-1. Blog Post with Links

```
{
        "id" : 1,
        "body" : "My first blog post",
        "postdate" : "2015-05-30T21:41:12.650Z",
        "links" : [
                {
                        "rel" : "self",
                        "href" : http://blog.example.com/posts/1,
                        "method" : "GET"
                }
        ]
}
```

In this response, each link in the links array contains three parts:

1. Href—Contains the URI that you can use to retrieve a resource or change the state of the application

2. Rel—Describes the relationship that the href link has with the current resource

3. Method—Indicates the HTTP method required to interact with the URI

From the link's href value, you can see that this is a self-referencing link. The rel element can contain arbitrary string values, and in this case, it has a value "self" to indicate this self-relationship. As discussed in Chapter 1, a resource can be identified by multiple URIs. In those situations, a self-link can be helpful to highlight the preferred canonical URI. In scenarios in which partial resource representations are returned (e.g., as part of a collection), including a self-link would allow a client to retrieve a full representation of the resource.

We can expand the blog post response to include other relationships. For example, each blog post has an author, the user that created the post. Each blog post also contains a set of related comments and tags. Listing 10-2 shows an example of a blog post representation with these additional link relationships.

Listing 10-2. Blog Post with Additional Relationships

```
{
        "id" : 1,
        "body" : "My first blog post",
        "postdate" : "2015-05-30T21:41:12.650Z",
        "self" : "http://blog.example.com/posts/1",
        "author" : "http://blog.example.com/profile/12345",
        "comments" : "http://blog.example.com/posts/1/comments",
        "tags" : "http://blog.example.com/posts/1/tags"
}
```

The resource representation in Listing 10-2 takes a different approach and doesn't use a links array. Instead, links to related resources are represented as JSON object properties. For example, the property with key author links the blog post with its creator. Similarly, the properties with keys comments and tags link the post with related comments and tags collection resources.

We used two different approaches for embedding HATEOAS links in a representation to highlight a lack of standardized linking within a JSON document. In both scenarios, the consuming clients can use the rel value to identify and navigate to the related resources. As long as the rel value doesn't change, the server can release new versions of the URI without breaking the client. It also makes it easy for consuming developers to explore the API without relying on heavy documentation.

HATEOAS DEBATE

The REST API for the QuickPoll application that we worked on so far doesn't follow the HATEOAS principles. The same applies to many public/open-source REST APIs being consumed today. In 2008, Roy Fielding expressed frustration in his blog (http://roy.gbiv.com/untangled/2008/rest-apis-must-be-hypertext-driven) at such APIs being called RESTful but that are not hypermedia-driven:

What needs to be done to make the REST architectural style clear on the notion that hypertext is a constraint? In other words, if the engine of application state (and hence the API) is not being driven by hypertext, then it cannot be RESTful and cannot be a REST API. Period. Is there some broken manual somewhere that needs to be fixed?

Seven years later, the debate around hypermedia's role and what is considered RESTful still continues. The blogosphere is filled with mixed opinions and people taking passionate stances on both sides. The so-called hypermedia skeptics feel that hypermedia is too academic and feel that adding extra links would bloat the payload and adds unnecessary complexity to support clients that really don't exist.

Kin Lane provides a good summary of the hypermedia debate in his blog post (`http://apievangelist.com/2014/08/05/the-hypermedia-api-debate-sorry-reasonable-just-does-not-sell/`).

JSON Hypermedia Types

To put it simply, a hypermedia type is a media type that contains well-defined semantics for linking resources. The HTML media type is a popular example of a hypermedia type. The JSON media type however doesn't provide native hyperlinking semantics and therefore is not considered to be a hypermedia type. This has resulted in a variety of custom implementations for embedding links in a JSON document. We have seen two approaches in the previous section.

Note   REST services that produce XML responses often use an Atom/AtomPub (`http://en.wikipedia.org/wiki/Atom_(standard)`) format for structuring HATEOAS links.

JSON Hypermedia Types

To address this issue and provide hyperlinking semantics within JSON documents, several JSON hypermedia types have been created:

- HAL—`http://stateless.co/hal_specification.html`
- JSON-LD—`http://json-ld.org`
- Collection+JSON—`http://amundsen.com/media-types/collection/`

- JSON API—http://jsonapi.org/

- Siren—https://github.com/kevinswiber/siren

HAL is one of the most popular hypermedia types and is supported by the Spring Framework. In the next section, we will cover the basics of HAL.

HAL

The **H**ypertext **A**pplication **L**anguage, or HAL, is a lean hypermedia type created by Mike Kelly in 2011. This specification supports both XML (application/hal+xml) and JSON (application/hal+json) formats.

The HAL media type defines a resource as a container of state, a collection of links, and a set of embedded resources. Figure 10-1 shows the HAL resource structure.

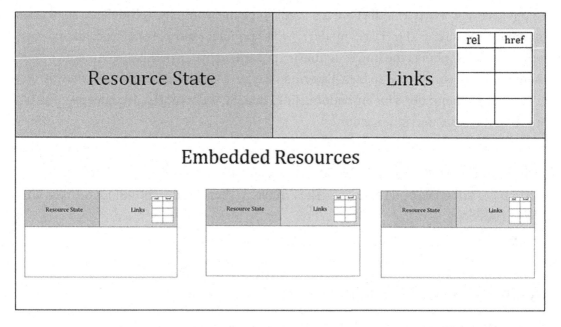

Figure 10-1. *HAL resource structure*

The resource state is expressed using JSON properties or key/value pairs. Listing 10-3 shows the state of a blog post resource.

Listing 10-3. Blog Post Resource State in HAL

```
{
        "id" : 1,
        "body" : "My first blog post",
        "postdate" : "2015-05-30T21:41:12.650Z"
}
```

The specification uses a reserved `_links` property to provide linking capabilities. The `_links` property is a JSON object that contains all of the links. Each link inside `_links` is keyed by their link relation with the value containing the URI and a set of optional properties. Listing 10-4 shows the blog post resource augmented with the `_links` property. Notice the usage of an additional property total count inside the `comments` link value.

Listing 10-4. Blog Post Resource with Links in HAL

```
{
        "id" : 1,
        "body" : "My first blog post",
        "postdate" : "2015-05-30T21:41:12.650Z",
        "_links" : {
                "self": { "href": "http://blog.example.com/posts/1" },
"comments": { "href": "http://blog.example.com/posts/1/comments",
"totalcount" : 20 },
                "tags": { "href": "http://blog.example.com/posts/1/tags" }
        }
}
```

There are situations in which it is more efficient to embed a resource than link to it. This would prevent the client from taking an extra round trip, allowing it to access the embedded resource directly. HAL uses a reserved `_embedded` property to embed resources. Each embedded resource is keyed by their link relation to the value containing the resource object. Listing 10-5 shows the blog post resource with an embedded author resource.

Listing 10-5. Blog Post Resource with Embedded Resource in HAL

```
{
        "id" : 1,
        "body" : "My first blog post",
        "postdate" : "2015-05-30T21:41:12.650Z",
        "_links" : {
                    "self": { "href": "http://blog.example.com/posts/1" },
"comments": { "href": "http://blog.example.com/posts/1/comments",
"totalcount" : 20 },
                    "tags": { "href": "http://blog.example.com/posts/1/
                    tags" }
        },
        "_embedded" : {
                        "author" : {
                          "_links" : {
                            "self": { "href": "http://blog.example.com/
                            profile/12345" }
                          },
                          "id" : 12345,
                          "name" : "John Doe",
                          "displayName" : "JDoe"
                          }
        }
}
```

HATEOAS in QuickPoll

The Spring Framework provides a Spring HATEOAS library that simplifies the creation of REST representations adhering to HATEOAS principles. Spring HATEOAS provides an API for creating links and assembling representations. In this section, we will use Spring HATEOAS to enrich the poll representation with the following three links:

- Self-referencing link

- Link to the votes collection resource

- Link to the ComputeResult resource

Note   The QuickPoll project that we are using in this chapter is available in the `Chapter10\starter` folder of the downloaded source code. To follow the instructions in this section, import the starter project into your IDE. The completed solution is available in the `Chapter10\final` folder. Please refer to that solution for complete code listings.

We begin the Spring HATEOAS integration by adding the Maven dependency shown in Listing 10-6 to the QuickPoll project's `pom.xml` file.

Listing 10-6. Spring HATEOAS Dependency

```
<dependency>
        <groupId>org.springframework.hateoas</groupId>
        <artifactId>spring-hateoas</artifactId>
        <version>1.3.3</version>
</dependency>
```

The next step is to modify the `Poll` Java class such that the generated representation has associated link information. To simplify embedding of hypermedia links, Spring HATEOAS provides an `org.springframework.hateoas.RepresentationModel` class that resource classes can extend. The `RepresentationModel` class contains several overloaded methods for adding and removing links. It also contains a `getId` method that returns the URI associated with the resource. The `getId` implementation adheres to the REST principle: the ID of a resource is its URI.

Listing 10-7 shows the modified `Poll` class extending `ResourceSupport`. If you remember, the `Poll` class already contains a `getId` method that returns the primary key associated with the corresponding database record. To accommodate the `getId` method introduced by the `RepresentationModel` base class, we refactored the `getId` and `setId` `Poll` class methods to `getPollId` and `setPollId`.

Listing 10-7. Modified Poll Class

```
package com.apress.domain;

import org.springframework.hateoas.RepresentationModel;

@Entity
public class Poll extends RepresentationModel {

        @Id
        @GeneratedValue
        @Column(name="POLL_ID")
        private Long id;

        @Column(name="QUESTION")
        private String question;

        @OneToMany(cascade=CascadeType.ALL)
        @JoinColumn(name="POLL_ID")
        @OrderBy
        private Set<Option> options;

        public Long getPollId() {
                return id;
        }
        public void setPollId(Long id) {
                this.id = id;
        }
        // Other Getters and Setter removed
}
```

In Chapter 4, we implemented PollController's createPoll method so that it constructed a URI of the newly created Poll resource using the getId method. The getId to getPollId refactoring just described requires us to update the createPoll method. Listing 10-8 shows the modified createPoll method using the getPollId method.

Listing 10-8. Modified createPoll() Method

```
@RequestMapping(value="/polls", method=RequestMethod.POST)
public ResponseEntity<?> createPoll(@RequestBody Poll poll) {
        poll = pollRepository.save(poll);

        // Set the location header for the newly created resource
        HttpHeaders responseHeaders = new HttpHeaders();

URI newPollUri = ServletUriComponentsBuilder.fromCurrentRequest().path
("/{id}").buildAndExpand(poll.getPollId()).toUri();
        responseHeaders.setLocation(newPollUri);

        return new ResponseEntity<>(null, responseHeaders, HttpStatus.
        CREATED);
}
```

Note   We modified our domain Poll class and had it extend the
RepresentationModel class. An alternative to this approach is to create a
new PollResource class to hold the Poll's representation and have it extend
the RepresentationModel class. With this approach, the Poll Java class
remains untouched. However, we need to modify the PollController so that
it copies the representation from each Poll to a PollResource and returns the
PollResource instances.

The final step in the Spring HATEOAS integration is to modify PollController
endpoints so that we can build links and inject them into responses. Listing 10-9 shows
the modified portions of the PollController.

Listing 10-9. PollController Modifications

```
package com.apress.controller;

import static org.springframework.hateoas.server.mvc.WebMvcLinkBuilder.
linkTo;
import static org.springframework.hateoas.server.mvc.WebMvcLinkBuilder.
methodOn;
```

```
@RestController
public class PollController {
        @RequestMapping(value="/polls", method=RequestMethod.GET)
        public ResponseEntity<Iterable<Poll>> getAllPolls() {
                Iterable<Poll> allPolls = pollRepository.findAll();
                for(Poll p : allPolls) {
                        updatePollResourceWithLinks(p);
                }
                return new ResponseEntity<>(allPolls, HttpStatus.OK);
        }

        @RequestMapping(value="/polls/{pollId}", method=RequestMethod.GET)
        public ResponseEntity<?> getPoll(@PathVariable Long pollId) {
                Optional<Poll> p = pollRepository.findById(pollId);
                if(!p.isPresent()) {
                        throw new Exception("Pool was not found");
                }
                updatePollResourceWithLinks(p.get());
                return new ResponseEntity<> (p.get(), HttpStatus.OK);
        }

        private void updatePollResourceWithLinks(Poll poll) {
poll.add(linkTo(methodOn(PollController.class).getAllPolls()).slash
(poll.getPollId()).withSelfRel());

poll.add(linkTo(methodOn(VoteController.class).getAllVotes(poll.
getPollId())).withRel("votes"));

poll.add(linkTo(methodOn(ComputeResultController.class).computeResult
(poll.getPollId())).withRel("compute-result"));
        }
}
```

Because links need to be generated and injected in multiple places, we created a updatePollResourceWithLinks method to hold the common code. Spring HATEOAS provides a convenient ControllerLinkBuilder class that can build links pointing to Spring MVC controllers. The updatePollResourceWithLinks method implementation uses the linkTo, methodOn, and slash utility methods. These methods are part of the Spring HATEOAS ControllerLinkBuilder class and can generate links pointing to Spring MVC controllers. The generated links are absolute URIs to resources. This relieves developers from having to look up server information such as protocol, hostname, port number, and so on, duplicating URI path strings (/polls) all over the place. To better understand these methods, let's dissect this code:

```
linkTo(
        methodOn(PollController.class).getAllPolls()
        )
        .slash(poll.getPollId())
        .withSelfRel()
```

The linkTo method can take a Spring MVC controller class or one of its methods as an argument. It then inspects the class or method for the @RequestMapping annotation and retrieves the path value to build the link. The methodOn method creates a dynamic proxy of the passed-in PollController class. When the getAllPolls method is invoked on the dynamic proxy, its @RequestMapping information is inspected and the value "/polls" is extracted. For methods such as getAllVotes that expect a parameter, we can pass in a null. However, if the parameter is used to build the URI, then a real value should be passed in.

The slash method, as the name suggests, appends the Poll's ID as a subresource to the current URI. Finally, the withSelfRel method instructs that the generated link should have a rel with value "self." Under the hood, the ControllerLinkBuilder class uses the ServletUriComponentsBuilder to obtain basic URI information such as hostname and builds the final URI. Hence, for a poll with ID 1, this code will generate the URI: http://localhost:8080/polls/1.

With these changes in place, run the QuickPoll application, and, using Postman, perform a GET request on the http://localhost:8080/polls URI. You will see that the generated response includes three links for each poll. Figure 10-2 shows the Postman request and partial response.

Figure 10-2. *Postman response with links*

Summary

In this chapter, we reviewed the HATEOAS constraint that enables developers to build flexible and loosely coupled APIs. We scratched the surface and used Spring HATEOAS to create QuickPoll REST representations that adhere to HATEOAS principles.

This brings us to the end of our journey. Throughout this book, you have learned the key features of REST and Spring technologies that simplify REST development. With this knowledge, you should be ready to start developing your own RESTful services. Happy coding!

Index

A, B

Amazon.com, 223
API implementation
  ComputeResult
    ComputeResultController class, 99
    DTOs, 98, 99
    endpoint test, 100
    output, 101
    votes count, 100
  PollController
    Content-Type header, 91
    createPoll method, 91, 92
    delete poll, 94
    fromCurrentRequest method, 91
    getAllPolls method, 89
    GET Verb, 89, 90
    individual poll, 93, 94
    inject dependency, 89
    JSON, 92
    message/headers, 93
    Postman, 90, 93
    @RequestBody, 91
    @RestController, 89
    ServletUriComponentsBuilder
      utility class, 91
    testing, 90
    update poll, 94, 95
    URI, 91
  VoteController, 95, 98
Aspect-oriented programming (AOP),
    21–24, 51
Authentication systems, 179

Authorization grant type, 178
Authorization server, 176

C

Cache, 2, 211
Certificate Authority (CA), 174
Client-server, 1
Code on demand, 2
Command line interface (CLI)
  command, 63
  contents, 62
  downloading, 62
  installation, 63
  output, 63
Content negotiation, 5
Controller resource, 13, 70
Create, Read, Update, and Delete
    (CRUD), 14
Cross-Site Request Forgery (CSRF),
    179, 194

D

Data-driven applications, 14
Dependency injection (DI), 23

E, F, G

Error handling, 103
  error messages
    createPoll method, 122
    handleValidationError, 122, 123

© Balaji Varanasi and Maxim Bartkov 2022
B. Varanasi and M. Bartkov, *Spring REST*, https://doi.org/10.1007/978-1-4842-7477-4

Error handling (*cont.*)
    messages.properties file, 122
    model_name, 122
    new message, 124
  error responses
    details, 107
    ErrorDetail class, 110
    GitHub, 108
    QuickPoll, 109, 110
    ResourceNotFoundException
      error, 111, 112
    RestExceptionHandler
      class, 110, 111
    Spring MVC components, 108
    Twilio, 108, 109
  getPoll implementation, 104, 105
  HTTP methods, 106
  input field validation
    Bean Validation API, 114
    custom error response, 120, 121
    updated ErrorDetail class, 117
    error key, 116
    error message, 116
    handleValidationError
      method, 118–120
    JSR 303/349, 113
    missing question, error code, 116
    options, 113
    poll class annotation, 114, 115
    PollController, @Valid annotations,
      115, 116
    poll creation, missing question,
      112, 113
    QuickPoll error response, 116
    RestExceptionHandler, 118
    updated ErrorDetail class, 118
    ValidationError class, 117, 118
    validation error format, 116, 117

  nonexistent poll, 103–106
  ResourceNotFoundException, 105
  RestExceptionHandler, 124–126
  Updated PollController, 106, 107

H

Hypermedia As The Engine Of Application
    State (HATEOAS)
  blog post resource, 224, 225
  blog post response, 225, 226
  JSON object properties, 226
  links array, 225
  QuickPoll
    ControllerLinkBuilder class, 235
    createPoll method, 232, 233
    getAllPolls method, 235
    links, 230
    linkTo method, 235
    methodOn method, 235
    Poll class, 231, 232
    PollController, 233, 234
    Postman response, 235
    RepresentationModel class,
      231, 233
    slash method, 235
    Spring dependency, 231
    updatePollResourceWithLinks
      method, 234
    withSelfRel method, 235
  REST API, 224, 226
  REST client, 224
  scenarios, 226
  Web, 224
Hamcrest, 212, 222
HTTP methods
  DELETE method, 9, 10
  GET method, 7, 8

HEAD method, 9
idempotency, 7
PATCH method, 13, 14
POST method, 12, 13
PUT method, 10, 11
safety, 7
status codes, 14–16
HTTP status codes, 107
Hypermedia As The Engine Of Application
State (HATEOAS), 236
Hypertext Application Language (HAL)
blog post resource, 228, 229
embedded resource, 229, 230
links, 229
_embedded property, 229
formats, 228
_links property, 229
structure, 228

I

Implicit grant type, 178, 179
Integration testing, 88, 211

J, K

Java ecosystem, 21, 211
Java Persistence API (JPA), 82
JavaScript Object Notation (JSON), 71
JSON hypermedia types, 227

L

Layered system, 2

M, N

Model View Controller (MVC), 24, 25

O

Open Authorization (OAuth), 176

P

Pagination
cursor-based, 158, 159
data, 159, 160
limit offset, 158
page number, 157
page size, 163–165
QuickPoll
configuration, 160
CrudRepository, 161
data subsets/informations, 161
findAll method, 161
getAllPolls method, 162
GET request, 162
import.sql file, 160
Pageable parameter, 162
paged results, metadata, 162, 163
PagingAndSortingRepository, 160
PollRepository, 161
Spring Data JPA, 160
time-based, 159
Password grant type, 178, 179
Postman, 64, 65

Q

QuickPoll
action identification
ComputeResult resource, 78
Poll resource, 76
Vote resource, 76, 77
API implementation (*see* API
implementation)
architecture, 78

QuickPoll (*cont.*)
   AuthenticationManagerBuilder, 192
   command, 192
   CRUD operations, 75
   cURL, 185
   domain implementation
      com.apress.domain, 83
      objects, 82, 83
      Option class, 83
      Poll class, 84
      Vote class, 85
   embedded database, 88
   endpoint identification, 74, 75
   error, 192
   Java client, 199, 200
   Postman, 184
   repository implementation, 85–87
   requirements, 69, 183
   resource identification, 69, 70
   resource representations
      ComputeResult, 74
      lists, 72, 73
      REST APIs, 71
      sample data, 72
      Vote, 73
   SecurityConfig class, 192
   security configuration, 191, 192
   service layer, 79
   Spring Boot, 184
   Spring Starter POM, 184
   spring starter project, 79–81
   URI
      command, 197
      cURL delete, 197
      DELETE HTTP method, 197
      deletePoll method, 194, 195
      EnableGlobalMethodSecurity, 194
      HttpSecurity parameter, 193

   permitAll method, 193
   Postman, 196
   @PreAuthorize, 195
   unauthorized response, 196
   WebSecurityConfigurer's config
      method, 192, 193
   user authentication, 183
   UserDetailsService implementation,
      189, 190
   user infrastructure setup
      testing, 187
      User class, 185
      user information, 188
      UserRepository, 187

R

REpresentational State Transfer (REST)
   clients, 157
   constraints/principles, 1, 2
   definition, 1
   representation, 5, 6
   resources, 3
      identification, 3, 4
      URI templates, 4, 5
   RESTful applications, 2
   Uniform Interface, 2
Resource server, 176, 178
RESTClient, 65, 66
RESTful API, 18
REST services
   approaches, 169
   certificate-based security model, 174
   digest authentication, 172, 173
   HTTP Basic authentication, 171, 172
   integration testing
      assertions, 222
      getAllPolls method, 220, 222

Hamcrest's hasSize matcher, 222

mocked MVC container, 220

Spring MVC Test framework, 220

vs. unit testing, 220

OAuth 2.0

authorization server, 177

Client, 177

client profiles, 178

definition, 176

HTTP POST, 177

HTTPS, 177

interaction, 177

public APIs, 177

response, 178

roles, 176

security flow, 176

tokens *vs.* access tokens, 179

session-based security model, 170

spring-test module, 212

@After annotation, 213

@Before annotation, 213

JUnit Test, 212, 213

libraries, 212

Maven dependency, 212

Spring Boot, 212

SpringJUnit4ClassRunner, 213

JUnit Test, 213

unit testing (*see* Unit testing)

XAuth, 174, 175

RestTemplate

authentication, 209, 211

DELETE method, 206

getting polls, 204

getForObject method, 202–204

getPollById method, 203

HTTP message converters, 202

List<Poll>.class, 203

ParameterizedTypeReference, 204

QuickPollClient class, 202, 203

URI template, 202

helper classes, 201

pagination

getAllPolls, 207

PageImpl, 207

PageWrapper Class, 207, 208

QuickPollClientV2 Class, 208, 209

poll creation, 205, 206

PUT method, 206

spring-web.jar file, 201

Richardson's Maturity Model
    (RMM), 16–18

S

Singleton resources, 4

Software as a Service (SaaS), 68

Sorting

ascending/descending, 165

QuickPoll, 166, 167

request, 165

REST services, 165

Spring Boot

annotations, 52

build tool, 46, 47

CLI (*see* Command line
    interface (CLI))

Hello World REST application, 48

contents, 48, 49, 53

greeting, 56

launching, 54, 55

main() method, 53

Maven-based Java project, 49

pom.xml file, 49–51

REST endpoint, 53, 54

opinionated approach, 45

options, 46

Spring Boot (*cont.*)
POM files, 51
starter modules, 51, 52
start.spring.io, 48
STS (*see* Spring Tool Suite (STS))
WAR artifacts, 49
Spring Framework modules, 22
Spring Initializr, 56
Spring portfolio projects, 22
Spring Security
AbstractSecurityInterceptor, 182
Authentication API, 180
AuthenticationManager, 181
AuthenticationProvider, 182
checking, 182
definition, 179
filter chain, 179
implementations, 181
request token, 180
SecurityContextHolder, 182
UserDetailsService API, 181
Spring Tool Suite (STS)
definition, 56
Spring Starter Project, 57
location, 60
Maven's GAV information, 57, 58
options, 59
resources, 61
website, 56
Spring Web MVC
architecture, 25–27
controllers, 27, 28
HandlerExceptionResolver
API, 39
@ControllerAdvice, 41
GlobalExceptionHandler, 41
handleSQLException method, 41
implementations, 39, 40

ResponseEntity, 40
SimpleMappingException
Resolver, 40
interceptors
addPathPatterns method, 44
HandlerInterceptor, 42
and HTTP servlet filters, 42
implementation, 43
InterceptorRegistry, 43
scenario, 42
model interface, 28, 29
path variables, 37
pattern, 24, 25
@RequestMapping
acccept header, 35
arguments, 35
Content-Type header, 35
elements, 32, 33
GET request, 34
POST method, 33
produces element, 34
return types, 36
shortcut annotations, 33, 34
@RequestParam, 31, 32
view, 29–31
ViewResolver, 37, 38
Swagger
API declaration file, 131, 132
api-docs, 130
configureSwagger method, 139
controllers
annotations, 145
@Api annotation, 140
@ApiOperation annotation,
141, 142
@ApiResponse annotation, 142, 143
createPoll method, 141
getPoll method, 142

PollController, 140
poll endpoint, 140
response messages, 143, 144
useDefaultResponseMessages
method, 144
createProduct, 131
customization
configureSwagger method, 138
Docket beans, 138
Docket, 137
implementation, 137, 138
includePattern method, 139
SwaggerConfig class, 138
updation, 138, 139
definition, 130
integration
api-docs, 133
Docket bean, 133, 134
resource listing file, 134, 135
springfox-boot-starter
dependency, 133
JSON, 130
resource file, 130, 131
UI, 135, 136

T

Traditional web applications, 169

U

Uniform Interface, 2, 6, 19
Unit testing, 211
DispatcherServlet, 215
findAll() method, 215
@Mock annotation, 215
PollController, 214, 215
Spring MVC Test framework

@Before annotated method, 219
classes, 216
content method, 217
getPolls method, 219
MockMvcBuilders class, 217
perform method, 217
PollControllerTest class, 219
post method, 216
POST HTTP request, 216
RequestBuilder parameter, 216
ResultActions, 217
testGetAllPolls method, 219
testGetAllPolls method, 215

V

Versioning
Accept header, 149
approaches, 148
custom header, 150
deprecation, API, 151
QuickPoll
approaches, 151
ComputeResultControler, 153, 154
packages, 152
PollController class, 152, 153
@RequestMapping, 153
Spring MVC, 152
VoteController, 153, 154
SwaggerConfig class, 154–156
URI, 148, 149
URI parameter, 149

W, X, Y, Z

Web Application Description Language
(WADL), 129
Web poll, 67, 68

Printed in the United States
by Baker & Taylor Publisher Services